Praise for *Ladies, LET'S NEGOTIATE*

"Women leave too much on the table when it comes to negotiating. Whether it's asking for a promotion, asking for a raise, or asking a partner to take on more responsibility at home, women settle for less than what's possible. Nan Gesche points women in the right direction with practical steps and stories of success. A must-read for women everywhere."

—Rita Webster, PhD,
founder and executive coach for women leaders at WiseLeader

"This is a must-read for women who may feel uncomfortable sitting at the negotiating table. Negotiation is not conflict; it is constructive problem-solving, and Nan Gesche provides all the tools to become a great listener who can arrive at win-win solutions."

—Susanne Lyons,
former chair of the US Olympic & Paralympic Committee,
former chief marketing officer of Charles Schwab, Inc. and VISA

"This is an important book for women in all areas of our lives. Negotiating is about more than the actual final agreement. It's about representing yourself in a way that proclaims your value, ideas, and positions. This book provides tools to assess, prepare, rehearse, and win!"

—Ann Johnson Stewart, PE,
MN senator and founder of PE Services

Ladies,

LET'S NEGOTIATE

HOW TO GO FROM FEAR TO FAIR

Nan Gesche

Ladies, Let's Negotiate © copyright 2026 by Nan Gesche. All rights reserved. No part of this book may be reproduced in any form whatsoever, by photography or xerography or by any other means, by broadcast or transmission, by translation into any kind of language, nor by recording electronically or otherwise, without permission in writing from the author, except by a reviewer, who may quote brief passages in critical articles or reviews.

ISBN 13: 978-1-63489-835-5
Library of Congress Catalog Number has been applied for.
Printed in the United States of America
First Printing: 2026

Cover design by Cori Lynch
Interior design by Dan Pitts
Author photo / Photography by Slow Road Photo
Edited by Kerry Stapley and Caitlin Fultz
Proofread by Karlee Steffanni and Abbie Phelps
Production editing by Lindsay Bohls

Wise Ink Media
PO Box 580195
Minneapolis, MN 55458-0195
wiseink.com

Wise Ink is a creative publishing agency for game-changers. Wise Ink authors uplift, inspire, and inform, and their titles support building a better and more equitable world. For more information, visit wiseink.com.

Contact Nan Gesche at nangesche.com for speaking engagements, training, coaching, and interviews.

For Rachel and Annika.

May you always move freely beyond fear.

CONTENTS

Author's Note   1
Introduction: Finding My Voice So You Can Find Yours   3

Part One: Prepare

1. Know Your Why: Define What You Want and Why It Matters   11
2. Shift Your Mindset: Move from Fear to Fair   19
3. Research: Prepare for Success   31
4. Script Your Start: Initiate with Impact   43

Part Two: Discuss

5. Open Strong: Build a Connection, Create Trust   55
6. Explore Options: Ask, Listen, and Understand   65
7. Advance Your Ask: Move Forward with Confidence   73
8. Rejection: Navigate the "No"   87

Part Three: Close

9. Sealing the Deal: Finalize Agreements   97
10. Follow-Through and Reflection: Build Skills for Next Time   103

Works Cited   109
About the Author   111

AUTHOR'S NOTE

"Nothing bad happens when women have more money."
—Sallie Krawcheck (former Ellevest CEO)

Many women are brilliant negotiators when negotiating for others. Yet we are more likely to falter when it comes to asking for ourselves. If we want more out of life, we need to learn to ask and negotiate for what we want. Whether you avoid negotiating like the plague or consider yourself at the top of your negotiation game, my hope is that this book will give you some practical tools to help you be more confident and capable.

While negotiations are often focused on money, that isn't the only thing that matters. You would be surprised (or not) by the number of women wanting tips on how to negotiate with their partner and their kids. This is the perfect place to start negotiating! We might have wanted to start out as the perfect wife or mother, only to discover that left us holding the chore bag. We don't need a research study to know that most women in opposite-sex marriages still do more housework and caregiving than men. (A 2023 Melbourne Institute study found that women do 23.1 hours of unpaid domestic work per week compared to 15.3 hours for men.) Ugh!

When teaching negotiations, I ask women how many hours they spend negotiating in a week. The typical answer is zero to five hours. Yes, some women say they *never* negotiate. Once you start to see how negotiations work, you might realize you have been missing opportunities to negotiate for a better life. You will start to see negotiation opportunities unfold in your everyday life with your kids, your parents, your partner, your coworkers, and others. My hope is that you create more opportunities to negotiate for yourself and to get more of what you want out of life.

Introduction

FINDING MY VOICE
SO YOU CAN FIND YOURS

"You get in life what you have the courage to ask for."
—Oprah Winfrey

Why Negotiations Matter for Women

I am not writing this book because I am a nationally recognized expert, nor have I negotiated hostage releases or won million-dollar deals. I'm writing this book because I have made some serious mistakes when it comes to protecting my own well-being. I've learned the hard way that negotiation is a skill we use every day, yet it is a skill that most of us never learned. For most of my life, I didn't realize I needed it—I didn't know what I didn't know.

My first job out of college was with the federal government. Salaries were transparent, and we all started at the same salary. The pay scales were openly shared, and we openly discussed our pay. There never seemed to be a reason to negotiate.

But everything changed when I realized that the story of women earning less than men had happened to me. About fifteen years ago, I discovered that one of my male coworkers was making almost $20,000 more a year, and we had the same job. I realized it took me nearly four years to earn what he made in three. If we both worked ten more years, he would make almost $200,000 more than I would. Imagine if I had taken that money and invested it at a 5 percent return for the next ten years—I would have $326,000. And that doesn't consider potential raises or the difference between our salaries the past ten years. If you took out your calculator and started doing hard math, I am pretty sure the cumulative effect was almost *half a million dollars* over twenty years. Yikes! I don't want this to be you!

How I Learned to Negotiate

After discovering the pay differential, there were two things I needed to do. First, I needed to understand how this happened and where I had missed the boat. Second, and more importantly, I needed to figure out how to make sure this didn't happen to me, or any other woman, again.

So, I asked my coworker if he could help me understand how this pay differential was created. His first comment was, "Well, you know, I did start a year before you, and I had a PhD." While both these statements were true, this only accounted for part of the difference.

Probing a bit further, it became clear that he had taken on a special project that wasn't required or openly offered to everyone. After a pause, I asked if there was anything else I should know about to understand the difference. Sheepishly, he said yes. "There was also that time I asked for a raise because my partner had gotten a raise and was now making more money than I was, so I got a little bump." *Dang*, this wasn't about fairness; it was about taking the risk to ask for more and to negotiate.

This discussion made it clear that I had to get serious about learning to negotiate—not just for myself but for my daughters, my sisters, my friends, or any other women who didn't want to end up in the same position. I dove into reading books, taking classes, and watching videos. It became an obsession.

The key takeaways from all this time and energy? Women lose out on opportunities for equal financial security.

- Women with advanced degrees are just as likely to negotiate as men, yet they still end up earning less than men ($0.83 for every $1.00 earned by men, with the disparity even larger for those who are Black, Indigenous, and people of color).

- Typically, men initiate salary negotiations more often than women do.

- When women negotiate, they typically ask for less money than men do.

- Women's reluctance to negotiate is more significant than most realize. Suppose you started working at twenty-three and got an estimated raise of 2 percent every year, while a peer negotiated a 3 percent raise every year. All other things equal—performance reviews, cost of living adjustments, and so on—you would end up earning 67.7 percent of what the other person was earning after forty years. Small differences at the start of your career compound into significant differences. (Keep in mind that pay inequities aren't due just to your negotiation skill levels. They are also due to bias, organization inequities, and more. This isn't all on you.)

- Women tend to underestimate their ability: Men think they need 50 to 70 percent of skills for a job application (and dating apps), while women think they need 70 percent or more.

- Women spend more time on unpaid or nonpromotable tasks than men. We are more likely to do work related to "office housekeeping"—organizing team events, collecting money for gifts, ordering lunch, providing emotional support to team members, mentoring new team members, and so on.

There are other costs of not negotiating; it's not just about the financial loss.

- Missed opportunities for special projects or a chance to develop additional skills

- Feeling tired or resentful due to not negotiating with your partner to create more equity in your load around the house or with the kids

- Missed opportunities to demonstrate negotiation skills to your kids or team members to set them up for a stronger future

The good news is that when women do negotiate, they're typically just as successful as men. This book is here to show you how to harness that power. Outlined below is the framework I now use when teaching other women how to negotiate.

The Negotiation Framework

- Prepare: 60 percent
    - Purpose: Clarify what you want and why it is important (WHY).
    - Attitude and Mindset: Identify what is holding you back and how to shift your perspective (WHY NOT).
    - Strategy/Research: Set the stage before you start (STRATEGY). Develop a plan based on research, preparation, and understanding your leverage.
    - Script Your Start—Reaching Out: Connect before you discuss and learn how to build a confident start (SCRIPT).
- Discuss: 30 percent
    - Open: Start the conversation and make a personal connection to set the tone for a collaborative negotiation.
    - Explore: Discover the other party's needs and concerns by asking questions and really listening.
    - Advance: Begin to bargain.
    - Objections and Rejections: Get past your partner's "No."

- Close: 10 percent
    - Agreement/Closure: Finalize your agreement, identify pitfalls, and confirm commitment.
    - Follow-Through and Reflection: Use each negotiation to learn how to do better next time.

This framework makes the process approachable. It provides practical steps that you can work through in segments. Whether you are negotiating a salary, setting boundaries, or sharing responsibilities, this book will build your skills and your confidence.

Think of negotiating like putting a puzzle together—there is a strategy. First, you pick out the puzzle: Identify your purpose and your desired outcome. Next, you lay all the pieces out on the table—this is your preparation. Then, select the outside pieces, and put them together to give the puzzle structure. You start to structure your interactions. You might sort the pieces by color or focus on the most vivid patterns, working through challenges piece by piece—like asking questions to uncover your negotiation partner's real issue. Some pieces will fall into place quickly, while others will require a lot of time and patience to figure out how they fit. This is the back-and-forth in the negotiation. Yet the puzzle isn't done until all the pieces are put into place. In a negotiation, that last piece means finalizing the agreement and taking time to reflect on your experience. Every negotiation is an opportunity to assess your skills and build your confidence for the next, perhaps bigger, puzzle.

Let's start putting the pieces together.

PART 1

Prepare

Preparation is more than the facts.
It is also about knowing yourself,
your values, and your voice.

Chapter 1

KNOW YOUR WHY:
DEFINE WHAT YOU WANT AND WHY IT MATTERS

> "Find your 'why' so that you have the strength
> and resilience to push through those times when
> everything else is telling you no."
>
> —Lisa Wimberger

My friend Jen had been working at her company for three years, consistently taking on additional responsibilities beyond her original job description. Her boss frequently praised her work, and her team relied on her to mentor new team members.

It was time for Jen's annual review, and I suggested she ask for a raise. After all, she had proven her value and wasn't at the top of her pay scale. But Jen hesitated.

"I don't want to seem ungrateful," she said. "My boss has been so supportive. What if asking for more makes things awkward between us? What if he thinks I'm only in this for the money?" She decided not to ask for a raise, as she didn't want to rock the boat. Instead, she accepted the standard 3 percent raise. She didn't mention the extra hours, the mentoring, or how her contributions had gone beyond her original role. She walked out of the meeting thrilled with her solid feedback and the great conversation with her boss about her future.

That held true until Jen found out a few months later that another team member who had started after her had negotiated a 6 percent raise in his review. "How did you do that?" Jen asked.

"I just laid out my contributions and how they've impacted the company. Our boss seemed to appreciate the detailed list of my contributions," Mark explained.

Jen was so irritated with herself—she had been worried about *the relationship over results,* assuming that advocating for herself would damage her relationship with her boss. What Jen didn't realize was that she could ask for what she wanted by demonstrating her worth *and* building on her relationship by providing her boss with the documentation to support her.

The Two R's of Negotiation—Results and Relationships

There are two R's to negotiation, no matter what you are negotiating for: results and relationships. When we negotiate for salary or a car, we often focus only on results. We are trained to get our economic interests met. When we negotiate with our family or friends, we often focus more on maintaining positive relationships. We are better served trying to focus on both. Neglecting either one can mean leaving value on the table or harming relationships, both of which can have long-term consequences for all parties.

Great negotiators refuse to believe that they have to choose between results and relationships. They understand that results are about getting your economic interests met or achieving your desired change. They also recognize that building relationships is a way of getting results.

Think about it. What would be the value of having a good relationship with your car dealer? Might you get a better deal? Might you find the experience more enjoyable? Might you have a resource should you have any issues with the car? Same with your family. Do you want less for them, or for yourself, in hopes of keeping peace? While it might seem harder to focus on both, once you get in the habit of focusing on both, you will find it is easier—with better outcomes for everyone involved.

Putting the R's into Practice

One of my favorite activities when I am teaching negotiations is asking people to talk about a problem that keeps them up at night. Participants have ninety seconds to share with their partner what the situation is from their perspective. While participants can vividly describe what is currently happening and why they are frustrated by the situation, few can clearly describe what a successful outcome looks like. It is the same for negotiations. This exercise makes clear a common problem in negotiation: clarity around goals.

Negotiations are like our GPS; we need both a starting and an ending point. We must know what our desired outcome is before we can start the negotiation conversation. While we may not get everything we ask for, we need to be clear about what we want in our ideal world.

Keep in mind that you can have multiple goals: getting a raise, setting boundaries, wanting to feel more respected, or setting examples for others. Set aside quality time to be clear about your goals. Stop settling for what people offer, and identify what you really want and need.

When I'm teaching negotiations, we make several attempts at clarifying our goals, starting with the questions at the end of the chapter. When you are finished with the first set of questions, you'll know half the story: your half. The next step is to try to consider the negotiation from the other party's perspective to think about your negotiation strategy. This way, you'll be prepared to present a win-win situation.

Imagine that your partner has lost their job or you realize you need to start saving to send your kids to college. While your boss probably does care about what is going on in your personal life, it is asking a lot to expect your boss to take your personal wants, needs, and desires to HR. Frame your ask around your contributions, market data, and the future value you bring the organization, and do it with confidence and calm. Think about the impact on your team from both a financial and a relationship perspective. That's reasoning your boss can get behind. (See chapter 3 on strategy.)

Negotiate Everyday Challenges

Start to negotiate everyday challenges to find a mutually agreeable solution. People often think that negotiations are just about money, but let me tell you, negotiating is a powerful tool when dealing with friends and family as well. My most vivid example was when my girls were young. I never felt like I had enough time when working full-time, and they didn't really want to help with chores around the house. I decided to practice my negotiation skills.

I asked my daughters if they'd like to spend more time with me doing fun things. Fortunately, when they agreed, I proposed, "Would you help me more around the house if I promise to spend more time with you doing fun things?" Watching their faces, I could see they weren't 100 percent sold, but I pressed on. I asked, "What if you got to pick your own chores?" They perked up some.

I sent them on their way, having asked them to find a list of things that a typical cleaning service might do. They were to review the list and pick out the things they thought we should be doing and which thing they might be willing to help with. We compared our lists to agree on chores that should be done and how often. They were then given the option to select five things they wanted to do on the list and tell me how often they would be willing to do them.

This entire process was a negotiation on what should be done, how often it should be done, and who was going to do it. We also negotiated some rewards for doing extra. We had a rule that the family was expected to help, that we didn't get paid for everything.

What I loved most about the process was that I was trying to teach my girls to problem-solve and negotiate. I wanted them to know they had a voice. Giving them that voice contributed to them actually doing their chores without having to be nagged or having to renegotiate every week.

Respect: The Bonus R

Remember that the goal is results *and* relationships, which leads to respect for all involved. Negotiation isn't only about getting exactly what you want; it's a chance to problem-solve together to find a solution that works for everyone.

Our behavior is deeply influenced by respect, inclusion, and acceptance. These values nurture self-esteem by making individuals feel heard and acknowledged. It is much easier to negotiate with these individuals than those who slip into ego-driven behavior, where the goal is to win at any cost, often at the expense of your dignity.

When fighting with your kids to go to bed, it isn't just about them getting enough sleep so they aren't crabby in the morning (although that is a pretty huge why). It is also about you getting some "me" time or time with your partner. Negotiations can reduce stress and improve the quality of your life. Knowing your why makes it easier to stay in the game. This holds true for bigger negotiations, such as boundaries, raises, shared responsibilities, respect, and more. Without a clear purpose, you might just be throwing darts at the wall hoping to hit the board. Without focus, you might end up with a lot of holes without accomplishing your goals.

Negotiation is about achieving results and strengthening relationships, which builds respect. By focusing on clear goals and thinking of the situation from the other party's perspective, you turn negotiations into a powerful tool for success in all areas of your life. Just remember while doing this that the main reason for the negotiation may be to improve the quality of your life and your relationships! There are plenty of negotiation opportunities around us every day that, if recognized, would improve the quality of our lives. Where do you want to start?

Visualize the Negotiation

You may have heard the comment "you have to see it to be it." Imagine you are a fly on the wall watching over the negotiation. How do you want it to unfold? What does the happy ending look like for all parties involved? If your purpose is fuzzy, you are less likely to achieve your goals. Recognize that the first concession you might be making is in your head before you walk into the room. Don't settle before you have even started the conversation. Ask for what you really want versus what you think you can get.

There are multiple ways to reach your goal, but you need to know what those goals are, or you will be spinning your wheels. Not only do you need to know them, but you also need to prioritize or weight them. List them all, then rank them for yourself and your negotiation partner.

APPLY THE PRACTICE

Defining Your Why

Take a moment to define what you want out of your negotiation. Be clear and specific.

Clarify Your Goals

- What is your main goal in this negotiation? (*Get a raise, create clear boundaries, create a flexible work schedule.*)

- Why is this goal important to you? (*Feel valued, better balance work and life, improve financial security.*)

- How will achieving this goal impact your future life or work? (*Increase job satisfaction, have more time with family, improve financial stability.*)

- If you could ask for anything without the fear of being rejected, what would you negotiate for? (*Don't overthink, just put something down. Don't sell yourself short!*)

- What would you be willing to compromise on if you can't get your ideal? (*If you can't have everything, what will you be willing to give up?*)

- What aren't you willing to compromise on? (*What are your deal-breakers? If you don't get this, you would walk away.*)

- What might be your fallback plan? (*This is where you start thinking about what you might take instead of your original request. See chapter 3 for more.*)

Consider Others' Goals

- What might be your negotiating partner's goal? (*What might be their why or why not?*)

- Why might this goal be important to them? (*reduce turnover, maintain engagement and relationships, watch their budget*)

- How might achieving the goal impact their future? (*Be seen as fair, get a promotion, achieve team recognition, avoid layoffs*)

- What might be the impact of not achieving their goal? (*experience turnover, go over budget, lay off staff, lose customers*)

Consider Relationships

- What do you want your relationship with your partner to look like when the negotiation ends? (*see improved problem-solving, more respect, the ability to tolerate each other*)

Chapter 2

SHIFT YOUR MINDSET:
MOVE FROM FEAR TO FAIR

"Don't bargain yourself down
before you get to the table."

—Carol Frohlinger

One of my first speaking engagements was with a group of women attorneys on "Why Women Don't Ask." One of the attorneys put me on trial before three minutes had passed, asking, "What makes you think we need to learn how to ask or to negotiate? I litigated for one of the biggest settlements in US history with big tobacco." My heart sank, and my brain seized up. I wanted to run out of that room and hide. What right did I have to teach a group of attorneys and litigators about asking for more?

Taking a deep breath to compose myself, I acknowledged they could probably teach me a lot about negotiating. Yet I knew I was there for a reason, so I asked them, "How many of you have negotiated for someone else in the past six months?" Every hand went up. Then I asked, "How many of you have negotiated for yourself in the last six months?" Only a couple of them raised their hands. Seeing this, one of the attorneys in the room spoke up on my behalf and said, "Maybe she has something to teach us, and I want to hear more."

Her reaction wasn't unique. Like many other women, our confidence in negotiating (or advocating) for others doesn't always translate into negotiating (or advocating) for ourselves. My thought was, "If they aren't willing to negotiate for themselves as skilled litigators, what hope is there for me?"

Discover What's Holding You Back

In the last chapter, we explored your "why," your reason for taking the risk to negotiate. This chapter is really about your "why not," the fear and doubts that might be holding you back. To move from *fear* to *fair*, you must figure out your fear—being seen as pushy, being rejected, looking stupid, feeling unworthy, or seeming as though you are asking for too much. You have to expose the fear to move past it.

This chapter is probably the most important chapter for me. As women, we negotiate for our coworkers, we negotiate for our teams, and we negotiate for our kids, yet we rarely negotiate just for ourselves. We must get into the mindset that we deserve to do this for ourselves. This often requires us to ask some hard questions to remind ourselves that fears aren't facts. We need to get out from behind ourselves and show up for ourselves. We need to figure out how to kick those fears to the curb if we want more. We need to turn off that crazy voice in our head telling us we can't.

Negotiation Doesn't Need to Be a Selfish Act

If you are paying attention to the other person and their needs, negotiations can be a win/win opportunity. The most effective negotiators allow their counterparts to be just as successful as themselves. It isn't me against you; it's thinking about how we make sure we're both successful.

Let me give you a very specific example. I was shoe shopping with some friends, and we went into one of our favorite stores. The gentleman behind the counter was rubbing his head like it was a tough day. When he didn't acknowledge us, I asked how he was doing. He responded that he thought he had the flu. I asked if anybody else was coming in to take his place so he could go home to rest. He flatly stated that no one else could come in.

We hustled our way to the clearance rack in the back of the store. Immediately we asked the clerk to get the matching shoes. You could tell he wasn't happy, so I sarcastically suggested he lock the door so nobody else could come in. He dryly said, "I did after you came in."

After trying on these shoes, we wanted him to get a few more. This time he was sitting on the couch, his elbows on his knees, again rubbing his head. He slowly got off the couch, clearly pained to be moving, and went to get the other shoes.

Looking at my friends, I explained that I was taking a class on negotiations. Our class homework was to negotiate something every day for a week. I asked if they were done enough until the next stop, as I wanted to try practicing my skills. They agreed. So, when the clerk came out of the back room with more boxes, I saw my chance. I looked at him and said, "I tell you what, if we don't ask for any more help, and we only buy from what you've already brought out for us, will you cut us a deal and give us an extra 50 percent off everything on the clearance rack?" He responded almost immediately with "Sure, as long as you don't ask for anything else." We scooped up the boxes of things we wanted and ran to the counter. As promised, he gave us an extra 50 percent off clearance items. I left with three pairs of Birkenstocks that were already 50 percent off for another 50 percent. I got three pairs of shoes for less than one cost originally! SCORE.

Keep in mind that the clerk also scored. By not asking for other shoes, we wrapped up our shopping earlier so he could close early and get some rest while still having decent sales that day. He moved older inventory by accepting the deal, shoes we might not have purchased without the extra discount. Because of this, we didn't take advantage of his illness. We worked together to both win.

We often think that people only care about money or about price. Yet many times when we go into negotiations, we have to pay attention to other people's emotions and needs. The salesclerk didn't care about the money; he just wanted us out of that store. His need to leave was far more important to him than getting full price for those Birkenstocks. Was it selfish to ask for something when it took the other person's needs into consideration? If the sale was more important than his well-being, he could have said no.

If I had thought he was only interested in price, I would never have asked to negotiate. A growth mindset is about seeing possibilities versus being limited to what we think is within our grasp to negotiate.

Our expectations, mindset, and attitude drive our behavior. If we assume it won't go well, it won't. Part of our preparation is to know how to calm our emotions and to identify what situations make it harder to manage our emotions. We need to learn how to breathe through those emotions so that we can maintain composure to push through that negotiation process. Instead of "I'm terrible at negotiating, and I don't know where to start," try "While I am not comfortable with negotiating *yet*, I can learn from each experience. Let's start learning." Here are some tips on how you might do that.

LEAD: Tips to Manage Your Emotions

L: Listen and Learn

With awareness comes change. You first have to learn to reconnect with yourself, not just what you are thinking. We each have to decide where we feel stuck and what we want to change.

- Listen to yourself to explore your emotions. When do you lose your courage to say what you feel or to ask for what you want? What is your internal voice telling you in those moments?

- Learn from those you respect. Listen to those who do negotiate effectively. What is their tone, their language, and their approach? What does it sound like, and what is the outcome?

E: Explore the Emotion

Fear and anxiety can reduce your effectiveness. To stay strong, you need to name the emotions and the underlying stories you might be telling yourself that aren't true.

- What emotions prevent you from negotiating for your wants?

- Fear often keeps us from taking risks. What are you afraid of? How likely is it that your fear is going to happen? What is the worst thing that could happen if that fear comes true? You may fear that in opening yourself up, you could be rejected, and this could make you feel undervalued or unloved.

- What identity are you most concerned about risking? This might be a fear of loss, the other person's anger, conflict, hurting someone, disapproval, rejection, and so on. You might be afraid that if you ask, you will be perceived as greedy or selfish, or that if you lose, you will not be seen as competent.

- Where are these feelings coming from? What makes you feel you are not entitled or worthy? The trick is to figure out what stops you in your tracks.

- Know your triggers.
    - What are the actions or behaviors by others that might cause you to go from 0 to 100? What things push your buttons and are more likely to cause you to react?
    - Remember that the calmer and more centered you are, the better you will be at handling difficult conversations like negotiations. Learning to manage your emotions will make it easier to manage shifts in the actual negotiation if there are differing perspectives (which is likely!).

A: Attitude Adjustment

If you don't have the right attitude, all the skills in the world will only get you so far. Reframing your thoughts can make a huge difference.

What do you need to do to come out from behind yourself? Have your feelings, or they will have you.

- Change how you label the experience: If we label negotiations as "stressful," we are more likely to feel nervous going into the conversation. If we think of negotiations as a normal conversation tool used to improve the situation for both you and your negotiation partner, it changes the entire dynamic. By approaching the situation positively, the energy you bring will also be positive.

- Visualize success: Think of what could go right rather than what could go wrong. Now that you know what story is creating these emotions, can you find a different story to tell yourself instead? What do you need to feel fully entitled to negotiate for yourself? What story would make you want to move forward?
    - Example: If your friend is getting paid more for the same job, and you do it just as well, you are not asking too much to be paid the same.

- Challenge your assumptions: Recognize that what you're feeling is not the only right emotion. Assumptions come from your beliefs and experiences, but that doesn't make them true.
    - Example: A friend was afraid to ask her grown son to move out for fear that it would hurt his feelings. When she had the discussion, she discovered he had been waiting for her to say it was okay.

- Function with fear: We have all learned to function when we are tired. If you have ever been a caregiver to kids, aging parents, or a sick partner, or if you have ever worked more than one full-time job, you know what I am talking about. You grab caffeine and make it happen. You power through.

You can do the same with negotiations. Think about where you might get that power.

- Example: When I was getting divorced, my attorney told me to get a mantra to tell myself when I felt like I was slipping into fear. She said she needed to hear my mantra at our next meeting. I came up with two: "I deserve as much as he does." "No one is above me or below me."

- Get back to the facts: What evidence do you have to support this attitude or story?
    - Example: We often dwell on that one bad experience. In the story at the start of the chapter I talk about when the attorney shook my confidence at the speaking engagement. One negative comment at one event doesn't define me and my ability.

- Remember, there are two sides to every story: You can't go into the negotiations with a "my way or the highway" attitude. Lean into the conversation with an open mind. Start from a place of curiosity and respect—for both yourself and the other person. Genuine respect and vulnerability typically produce more of the same.

D: Do Something

Here are practical strategies for managing your nerves. Do these things before you need to so you can pull them out of your pocket when the opportunity arises.

- Support yourself: What do you need to do to feel your most calm or confident in these situations? This could be a power outfit, a good night's rest and healthy breakfast, or ten minutes of silence to meditate or breathe. What works for you?

- Build your immunity to fear: Practice, practice, practice. Each time you do this, it gets easier. Instead of avoiding negotiations, build strength in small doses. Find small risks to build your courage and expand your ability to deal with discomfort. You negotiate for $1 today and $10,000 in a year.

- What one small thing can you negotiate today?
- How will you track your wins to learn from the experience?
- What will you do differently next time?

- Breathe: Emotions crash into us like waves on a beach; we just need to ride the wave without reacting because the emotion will recede. When we can learn to create some space in our brain, we can stay better focused on our goal.

  - What is your go-to calming technique you can use before negotiating?
  - How do you remind yourself it is okay to feel nervous?

- Practice your power pose: Our nonverbals often say more than our words. Find an action that makes you feel powerful. When I was taking coaching classes, we were told to think of ourselves as dragons with sturdy tails for support, a tall, solid body, and big feet to ground us. A power pose can be anything that brings you confidence.

- Be ready to compromise: If you already have your solution in mind, there's nowhere for the conversation to go. Challenge your own assumptions and beliefs. What might change your mind about the situation?

- Check your ego: If you need to win or prove you're right, you might check this mindset at the door. This isn't a battle to be won—it is a problem to solve together.

- Know your values: The clearer you are about your top two to three core values, the easier it will be to stick to them. If you aren't sure of your top couple of values, start by making a list of your top eight to ten values from any value list on the internet. Narrow the list to your top five values. Reflect and come back to your top three.

Have a conversation with yourself. Understand why you might be settling. Once you're aware of the stories you're telling yourself, you can reframe them and determine how to create something better for yourself. Remember that the more comfortable you are, the more likely it is you will make your partners comfortable, which increases the likelihood of a successful agreement.

Shifting "from fear to fair" is about remembering your worth and turning off your inner critic. The only way you will get better is to start practicing. Change happens one step at a time. Below are a few ways you can apply LEAD to scenarios at work and in your personal life.

LEAD Examples: Listen, Explore, Attitude Adjustment, Do Something

At Work: Asking for a Raise

L What has changed since your last review?
E What fear is holding you back? Fear of being seen as "greedy"?
A Frame your request: "This is the additional value I have contributed."
D Prepare market data to support your ask, and practice asking with a friend.

At Home: Asking Your Partner to Help More with Chores

L What makes you afraid to ask?
E Are you afraid of rejection? Starting a conflict?
A Think about your ask: "I'd like us to better share responsibilities."
D Find a time to discuss. Negotiate a couple of small changes you might try.

With Friends:
Setting a Boundary with a Friend Who Is Late

L How do you feel when your friend is late?

E What's the worst thing that could happen if you bring this up?

A What is the best thing that could happen? "When we are late for reservations, it stresses me out. I would like to find a realistic meeting time so we aren't late."

D If it happens again, reinforce your boundary by stating you are unable to attend events going forward.

Reduce your stress, preserve your sanity, and improve the quality of your life.

APPLY THE PRACTICE

Attitude Adjustment—Your Why Not

Identify what has held you back from negotiating and reframe your fears into positive statements.

- List three fears you have going into this negotiation. (*being seen as greedy, facing rejection, not knowing what to say*)

- Reframe each fear into a positive statement. (*"My needs are as important as others'." "Rejection is a step toward the right direction." "Preparation is my superpower."*)

- What besides fear has held you back from negotiating in the past? (*putting others' needs before my own, couldn't speak to my own need, didn't know what I didn't know*)

- Write down one strategy you will use to stay confident. (*One of my favorite strategies is choosing a mantra.*)

- Write down a mantra that keeps you grounded and will help you move forward. (*"I have the right to ask for what I want." "No one is above me or below me."*)

Chapter 3

RESEARCH:
PREPARE FOR SUCCESS

"You need to do your homework. A negotiation is the time for you to show others how you value yourself and advocate for yourself."

—Catalina Rojas

Hi Nan,

I participated in your virtual learning from WiM (Women in Manufacturing) for "Ladies, Let's Negotiate" one month ago. I was so inspired by your strategy (and frankly frustrated with no annual raises this year for my company). I did exactly what you suggested. First, I prepped my evidence—my work, responsibilities, and projects, as well as salary comps both inside and outside of my organization. Then I laid out my range—salary values but also a PTO ask in case salary was completely not doable. Finally, I jotted down my possible responses for the conversation. Then I was ready to schedule my 1:1 with HR. The meeting went swimmingly, and HR was very open to an increase. It took a few weeks, but last Friday I was given a salary increase of 9.1 percent, which is honestly way more than I would have asked for if I had been forced to give a number. My husband and I were celebrating, and he said, "I'm proud of you for being so brave and asking for it." My response was to thank Nan and the WiM webinar for the inspiration and courage.

So I just wanted to share my success story and personally say "Thank you, Nan!" You are doing amazing work that women need to hear because we do not naturally want to negotiate. I'm sure that I am one of many that your words have helped out.

Have a wonderful week!

Amanda

Amanda's success wasn't just about bravery—it was about preparation. She knew her purpose (her why), she was motivated (which got her past her why not), and she did her homework to be competent during the negotiation process. She had a strategy for preparing for the conversation; she set the stage in advance to make herself more comfortable and confident. She built the edges of her puzzle. Let's explore how you can do the same.

Do Your Research!

Amanda's success was not by chance. She built her credibility by researching the market, documenting her strengths, and considering the company perspective. She positioned herself as a confident, informed negotiator. She prepared in hopes of finding the Zone of Possible Agreement (ZOPA).

ZOPA–Zone of Possible Agreement

Estimate Your ZOPA

Your ZOPA is the overlap between what you and your negotiating partner want. Your ZOPA is nothing more than your bargain zone. It is based on the belief that there is some range of possible outcomes that you and your partner can agree to. It is about identifying where you and your partner might be willing to compromise. Finding this zone is one of the first steps of the actual negotiation. Once you have a range, it is easier to negotiate until you can reach an agreeable compromise.

Bringing your range of possible agreements at the beginning of a negotiation will make you more confident. It also puts you in the mindset that this is a give-and-take conversation. Knowing where you can give in the discussion makes it easy to offer something to your partner, which in turn will signal to your partner that there is some wiggle room.

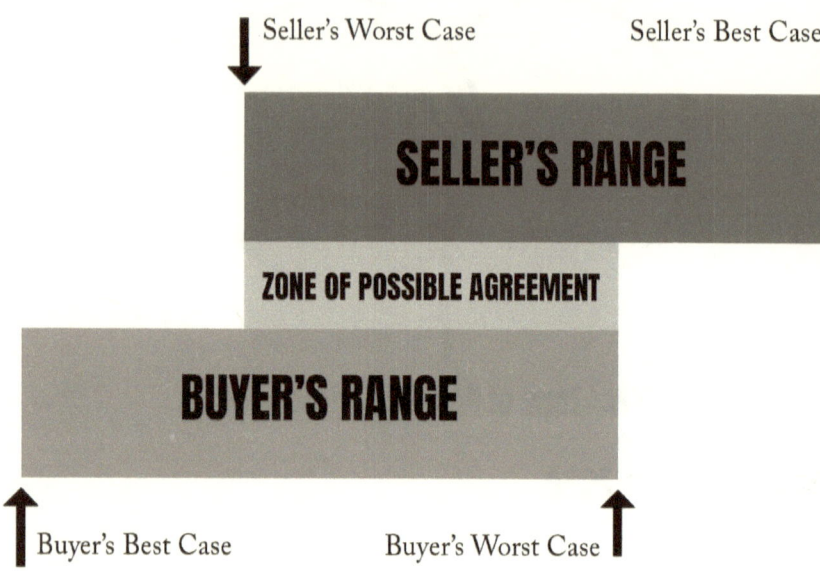

The data or options you gather to find your ZOPA will depend on what you are negotiating. If you are negotiating salary, you will want to gather data externally from sources outside the company as well as internally.

External (outside of your organization or group):

- Leverage market research. Amanda used a variety of resources to find what her skill set was worth. She looked up job postings and salary ranges to determine her market value.

- How many empty positions are currently open in the market? Could she easily find another job doing the same work? What is the demand for her skills in the open market?

Internal (within your organization or group):

- How easy would it be to fill her current job? What specialized skills does she have that might be difficult to replace?

- What information does she have about her contributions to her team or the organization? (Amanda kept a file on her contributions to the organization. Don't assume anyone else is keeping track of this for you.)

While I can't promise the results that Amanda got, following a strategy will put you in a better position than most when you go into the conversation. Once you are clear on your purpose and have shaken off any silly story as to why you can't, now's the time to roll up your sleeves to get to specifics of the actual negotiation discussion.

Three Parts to Research

There are three parts to research: self (see chapter 2), others, and market/standard/policy.

Strategy: Do Your Research

Yourself	Others	Market

• What is your style?
 • Who are you really negotiating for?
 • What do you really want?
    - Goals/Outcomes
    - Relationship
    - Consequences you can live with
 • How have you let them down?
 • What do you have to leverage?
 • What are your options?
	• What is their style?
	 • What are their needs, wants, and interests?
	 • What are their other options?
	 • What might be the ZOPA?
		• What comparable data do you have?
		 • What are the reasonable parameters given the market?
		 • What are reasonable options or alternatives?
		 • What things might you bundle in the negotiation?

Self

Having a purpose isn't enough. There is a lot of other information you need to get started. Think through these things before you consider scheduling a meeting:

- **Aspiration or Ideal**: If you could ask for anything in the world without risking the relationship, what would you ask for? It is easier to negotiate down from a high number than up from a lower one. Ask for more than you want, within reason, given your research.

- **Bottom Line**: This is the minimum you are willing to accept. Anything below this is worse than not negotiating at all. You will feel like you lost if you go below this.

- **Leverage**: Options create strength. Options aren't just fallback plans—they strengthen your position. The more alternatives you have, the more confident and better position you have. (Like your GPS navigation system, the more options you have to get to your destination, the less likely you will get stuck or be late.) Here are some examples:
    - Raise/Promotion: Other job offers, specialized skills, meeting or exceeding education requirements, a strong professional network, high market demand, documented history of strong performance.
    - Car Purchase: Knowing the market value of the car, being open to different models or different dealers, avoiding rushing the decision, being willing to accept different features.
    - Help at Home: Hiring a cleaner, subscribing to a meal prep service, redistributing tasks based on preferences, automating or simplifying regular tasks, lowering your standards.

- Aging Parents Driving: Senior citizen services, Uber/Lyft, paying friends/neighbors to drive, carpooling to regular social events.

- **Best Reasons**: Identify your three best reasons why you think you deserve what you are asking for.

- **Communication Style**: What is your style, and how might that impact the process? Women face what is called the double bind where we must balance likability with competence and credibility more than men. While it is important to be authentic to your own style, you also need to consider the following:

    - Language: The words you use impact people's perceptions. Be inclusive by using "we" or "us" language. Advocate for yourself, and on behalf of your team, the organization, or a client.

    - Tone: Know your tone. As odd as it sounds, we may hear tone in others yet be tone-deaf to our own voice. Ask friends and coworkers when they notice your tone shifts, especially ones that may be less desirable. Once you are aware of these situations, you can plan how you'll adjust your tone.

    - Pace: Slow down your pace to a more relaxed speed, especially if you tend to be a fast talker.

    - Body Language: Don't be afraid to take a seat at the table rather than along the wall in meetings. Spread out and claim your space. Avoid nodding too much, as it may signal too much agreement, which could weaken your position. Use your power pose.

Others

Understanding yourself is only the first part of the equation; you also must understand your negotiating partner. Successful negotiation is as much, if not more, about understanding the other party. Amanda took the time to consider the company's perspective, goals, and constraints. After all, no one had gotten a raise in the past year. She had to think about what the company was getting in return for paying her a higher salary.

If you haven't built a relationship with your negotiation partner, you will have to do some research.

- **Their Ideal**: What might be the other person's ideal? What do they value? For example, knowing what skills and qualities a hiring manager wants will help you highlight what you bring to the table, thus minimizing resistance to requests for more money.

- **Their Bottom Line**: What might be their bottom line? What constraints might they be facing?

- **Their Options**: What other options might they have? You want to consider this, as this can have a huge impact on your discussion. Remember, the more options they have, the less flexible they might be during the negotiation. Identifying as many options as possible will help you maximize value for you both and increase the likelihood of a successful outcome.

- **Their Objections**: A key part of Amanda's preparation was anticipating potential objections. She made a list of possible negative reactions and scripted her replies. This proactive approach ensured that she was not caught off guard during the negotiation and could address concerns calmly and effectively. You probably won't think of every objection, but preparing for the most likely ones will keep you calm and more prepared for whatever might come your way.

    - Make a list of all the possible negative reactions that can come up in the discussion. If you know your vulnerabilities in advance, you can plan to compensate for them.

- Label the feeling or possible reaction to the negative item. For example, if you missed a deadline, your supervisor might think you are undependable.

- Script how you might address the feeling. How can you own this? What words could you use to acknowledge their objections? For example, "I might seem like I am unreliable, and you might not think I deserve a raise because of this. Here is what I have done to address the issue." While there is no guarantee that this won't be held against you, it will help them focus on solutions rather than negative feelings. Negative feelings are stronger than positive feelings, so help them get rid of the negative emotions.

- **Their Leverage**: What might they have to leverage? They have more leverage if there are multiple candidates who can fill your job or the car you want is the last one on the lot. What solutions might they want you to consider?

- **Their Style**: What is their style, and how might that impact the process? How do you stay calm should they become irritated or angry?

Data/Market

Look beyond you and your partner. It is also important to understand what is going on around you—across the market, in your industry, or at least down the hall.

Let me give you a quick story to make this point. My daughter received notice of a rent increase and went into action.

- She researched vacancy rates, average rents for similar units nearby, and recent ads (including promotions) from her own complex.

- She put all the information onto a one-page summary.

- She scripted her opening line: "I'd like to renew my lease. Based on current vacancy rates, nearby listings, and ads from this complex showing cost with signing perks (one month free / reduced deposits), could we keep my rent at X dollars if I sign a twelve-month lease?"

- She stayed positive while sharing the data and reinforced that she had been a reliable tenant. The outcome: no rent increase.

Data can transform what feels like a hard conversation into a low-stress proposal. Consider gathering:

- **Comparable Data**: Look for internal and external salary information, use industry surveys, local comps (rentals, service rates, product pricing, salaries). What are competitors offering beyond salary or price?

- **Reasonable Ranges**: What is realistic given the market (unemployment rates, product inventory, budget cycles)?

- **Options in the Market**: What other options exist in the market (alternative suppliers, listings, models, timing)?

- **Your Track Record**: What data have you kept on yourself? Pro tip: Keep an Awesome File on yourself if you are considering asking for a raise or promotion, to justify the top of your range or just to remind yourself of the great job you have done should you start to lose your courage!

APPLY THE PRACTICE

There is little you can control once the negotiation conversation starts except your preparation. A good strategy is like your safety net. It gives you something to fall back on when you move into the conversation. Knowing your goals, getting in the right frame of mind, exploring options, and drafting responses will help build your confidence before you enter the room. Preparation is *everything*!

Strategy Preparation

Create your negotiation strategy to build credibility and confidence.

Define Your Position

- What's your ideal outcome?

- What's your starting offer? (*Request a 15 percent raise to negotiate down to your ideal, say 10 percent.*)

- What's your minimum acceptable outcome?

- What aren't you willing to compromise on? What is a deal-breaker?

Build Your Case

- List your three strongest reasons to support your request.

Anticipate Objections

- List potential objections you think your partner might make.

APPLY THE PRACTICE

- How will you respond? Script possible responses. *("You might think I am unreliable, and you might also think I don't deserve a raise because of this. Here is what I have done to address the issue . . . ")*

- What additional support might you need to counter the objection?

Identify Backup Options

- Identify other things you can ask for if your initial request is rejected. *(additional vacation days, training or development opportunities)*

- Explore alternatives available to you. *(buying a different car at the dealer down the street)*

Cultivate Your Communication Style

Before you enter the room, set your intention for how you'll show up:

- Language: Identify words/phrases you want to use to advocate for yourself while framing benefits for others.

- Tone: Consider the tone you want to maintain, assertive and warm.

- Pace: What will you do to keep from rushing?

- Body language: What movements do you want to avoid or enhance to reflect confidence?

Chapter 4

SCRIPT YOUR START:
INITIATE WITH IMPACT

"Ask for what you want and be prepared to get it."
—Maya Angelou

Your day is going great until someone stops you in the hallway and says, "Can we talk?"

You get a sick feeling in your stomach, and your mind begins to race. *What did I do wrong? Did I miss something?* You get the feeling that something big is going to happen and it isn't going to be good. Have you ever experienced this? I know I have, and it wasn't a pleasant feeling.

The problem with this type of start to a negotiation is that it could leave your partner feeling tense, on edge, and even defensive. This isn't a great way to start any conversation. Instead, script your start to set a cooperative tone. Set the stage so that your partner has a chance to mentally and emotionally prepare for the conversation just as you have in hopes that they can bring their best self to the table and fully engage in a productive manner.

The Meeting Before the Meeting

An often-overlooked step in negotiations is what I call "the meeting before the meeting." After you have done your research, now it is time to reach out to your partner to signal that you would like to negotiate. This isn't the negotiation itself; rather, it is taking time to set the stage. It is a quick pre-meeting chat or email to set up the actual negotiation.

In an ideal world, you don't just jump into most negotiations. If you want your partner to be more relaxed during the negotiation, you also give them time to prepare for the negotiation. You can create goodwill and trust by setting the negotiating process before the actual negotiation to signal that you are open to considering their wants, needs, and interests. This sets a tone of mutual respect and communicates that you are committed to a cooperative process.

Here is how to set the stage effectively:

- Clearly State Your Purpose: Reach out to your partner to let them know in advance that you want to negotiate something. Be as clear about the topic as possible. For example: "I'd like to discuss how we might restructure my workload." "I'd like to have a conversation about how we share responsibilities around the house."

- Work Out the Logistics: Take some time to work out the logistics of your actual negotiation meeting together. This reinforces collaboration and respect. Recognize that if you are in a power position, you need to be open to allowing them more control over some of the meeting logistics:

    - What: The main goal of the negotiation.

    - When: The time that works best for both of you.

    - Where: A place that feels neutral to you both that also minimizes distractions and interruptions. Ideally negotiations are done in person, especially the first meeting.

    - Who: Identify who else might need to attend.

    - How: Set any ground rules or expectations for the conversation, such as confidentiality, the length of the meeting, and how you might structure your time together. If time is limited, consider setting a second meeting date.

- Signal Your Openness: I was once told "Every possible disagreement is best started with an agreement." Use the meeting before the meeting to show your flexibility. Ask for their preferences and accommodate when possible. This small gesture will model the type of interaction you want in the negotiation itself.

By taking the time to align on logistics, establish an agenda, and signal your willingness to collaborate, you demonstrate professionalism and respect. The meeting before the meeting is your opportunity to ensure the actual negotiation begins on a foundation of trust, clarity, and shared purpose. This sets the stage for building common ground to start and keep the negotiation moving forward.

Here's a real-world example of reaching out first: During a recession, a bank reached out to me to discuss how to get its customers to come in to talk about restructuring their loans. Borrowers were falling behind in their payments and were at risk of losing their property. Few bankers want to repossess property, because when they do, they aren't getting paid, they have to insure the item, and they have to market and carry the cost of maintenance/storage until the item is sold.

The bankers couldn't figure out why no one was coming into the bank to discuss their missed payments and possibly restructure their loans. Well, most people don't want to reach out to negotiate, especially when they know they are part of the problem. It's intimidating and embarrassing.

Instead of waiting for the customer to come to the bank, I suggested the loan officers might reach out to each customer to let them know they were interested in renegotiating the terms of their loan. Someone had to start the conversation, and reaching out first would signal that the bank was willing to work with the customer. Next, I suggested they have the customer select the time and place of the meeting.

These simple changes set the tone for a collaborative negotiation. No surprise, the bank was able to significantly increase the number of loans renegotiated while allowing its customers to save face in their community. Everyone benefited.

Build Common Ground: Make a Personal Connection

A big part of negotiations is building a trusting relationship. You need to signal that you care about the other person as an individual as well as about the outcome of the conversation. Remember, it is about relationships and results. You don't want to just dive into the conversation without some connection.

Ask yourself:

- What do you know about them personally that you can use to connect at the start of the conversation?

- Go back to any shared purpose. What is something you both care about?

- What information are you willing to share that might shift the conversation?

Negotiations aren't just about facts; they are also about emotions. Remember my Birkenstock story? The salesclerk wasn't interested in just sales—he was interested in going home to bed. Even a small connection, made by asking questions to understand their current situation, can build trust and soften resistance.

Script Out Responses to Possible Rejections

This is a good time to go back to your research. Think about the reasons why someone would or would not want to give you what you are asking for. Consider what concerns they might raise.

Think about how you might answer their objections and script out a possible response.

For example, a business partner may feel cheated on price negotiation. "I know you found a cheaper price once I promised we had the best deal. While our price didn't end up being as competitive as we hoped, we did deliver on all other promises. What do you need to make this right?"

Script Your Start of the Negotiation

My mother's husband was suffering from dementia. This kind and gentle man was turning into someone we didn't recognize. This was a man who had a plan and worked the plan, mapping out every travel stop. A week's trip could be pages of information with the contact information for every stop along the way.

Well, things were changing. On several occasions, he got lost when driving. Thankfully my mother was usually with him and could gently guide him home. Then there was the trip to the mall by himself when he couldn't remember where he'd parked the car. Mom knew it was time to hide the keys, yet somehow, he would find them.

When my sisters and I got the news that they had been in a car accident—luckily no one was hurt—we all knew it was time to have a hard conversation. We agreed that the car should be sold, or we needed to find a better way to secure the car keys. We also knew it wasn't our decision—it was theirs. We had to negotiate with our mother.

Knowing what should happen and having the conversation on how to handle the situation are two different things. When we confronted our mother, we made it clear we were concerned about their safety. We loved them both, and we didn't want them hurt. Her response surprised us: "Well, if we die, we will go together." Alarm bells were going off in my head. I had to ask, "What if someone else was hurt? How would that feel to live with the fact that someone else had been injured or killed?"

One would think this is an easy and logical conversation. Yet if you have been in this position, you know it isn't. This is a negotiation because the other person gets to make the final decision. Until a doctor or those issuing licenses say they aren't fit, you can only try to negotiate a different way of behaving.

In a situation like this, you could say, "Mom, I know your freedom is important to you and your husband. Recent events have me concerned for your safety and the safety of others. I wanted to hear what you think about the situation and any ideas on how to keep everyone safe."

More sample scripts:

- Asking for a raise (Amanda's story in chapter 3): "Thanks for taking the time out of your schedule to talk with me. Given everything that I have accomplished this past year, I would like to explore the possibility of a raise. I have some things I would like to share during the discussion, and I also want to hear your perspective."

- Declining an extra project: "I know that quality is important to you, and I know this project needs my full attention. Right now, my plate is full, and I am not sure I can give the project the attention it needs to deliver the kind of product you or the customer deserves. Could we find a time to discuss how both our needs could be met?"

The Power of Practice

It isn't enough to write your script. You also need to practice it.

- Say it out loud: Things sometimes sound different out loud than they do on paper. By practicing, you can decide if the wording is comfortable. Does it really sound like you and roll off your tongue?

- Watch your body language: Practice in front of the mirror to see if you are smiling, making eye contact, or slouching like you aren't sure. Your nonverbal cues matter as much as your words.

- Practice with a friend: Ask a friend to role-play or listen to your opening comments so you can watch their reaction. Then ask:
    - What parts felt solid?
    - Where was I unclear or seemingly uncertain?
    - What advice do you have for improvement?
    - Where might you reject what I am saying?

- Visualize a positive outcome: To boost your confidence, visualize what could go right. The calmer and more focused you are, the easier it will be to slow down your pace, which helps you come across as composed, credible, and likable.

Once you've practiced your script, you're not done yet. Strong negotiators come prepared with smart questions that help keep the conversation focused.

Questions

Develop three to five questions to guide you through the discussion and keep you grounded. After the meeting before the meeting, script your first few sentences to start the actual negotiation. Stop and consider what information might be needed to move the conversation forward and decide your next course of action.

- What does success look like for you?
- What do you consider a deal-breaker?
- What would you be willing to give up to ensure you get what is most important to you?

APPLY THE PRACTICE

APPLY THE PRACTICE
Scripting Your Start

Use the provided template to draft your own meeting before the meeting.

Purpose

- What's your main goal?

    "I'd like to discuss adjusting my salary to better reflect my contributions to the team."

- How will you build common ground?

    "I know we both want our team to be successful and run smoothly."

- What positive framing can you use?

    "I'm excited about the progress we've made, and I'd like to explore how we can keep building on that."

Logistics

Working together to structure the meeting sets a collaborative tone.

- **When?** When is a good time for them?

- **Where?** Ideally this is done in person at a private, neutral location.

- **Who?** Besides you and your partner, who else might need to attend?

- **How?** What ground rules might you put into place? Consider the length of the meeting and how you might structure the meeting.

Role-Play

- Practice with a partner. Ask a friend or family member to role-play with you.

- Ask for feedback.
    - *"What felt strong, or where did I seem confident?"*
    - *"Where did I seem nervous or stumble?"*
    - *"What can I adjust to strengthen my start?"*

By scripting your start and practicing, you set the stage for a less stressful and more collaborative negotiation.

PART 2

Discuss

Negotiation is a conversation where connection and curiosity are key.

Chapter 5

OPEN STRONG:
BUILD A CONNECTION, CREATE TRUST

> "For most women, the language of conversation is primarily a language of rapport: a way of establishing connections and negotiating relationships."
>
> —Deborah Tannen

My kids used to cringe when I struck up a conversation with a random stranger. Whether it was a quick comment about a long wait for something, a remark about their shoes, or some observation about the moment, it was my way of breaking the ice and building micro-connections.

Building rapport is many women's greatest superpower, and it often starts with simple gestures like outlined above. While nature may be at play here, nurture also has a hand. We have been taught to find common ground, prioritize relationships, and make connections. By focusing on relationships and shared goals, we build trust to turn challenges into opportunities.

Rapport: The Importance of Human Connection

Have you ever had a conversation where it felt like the other person saw you only as an obstacle to getting what they wanted? Where they treated you like you were a nuisance and seemed to have no interest in you or your needs? They're not exactly the person you want to negotiate with. Now think about the people you can say anything to. What makes them different?

According to Robert B. Cialdini in his book *Influence: The Psychology of Persuasion*, one of the keys to persuading and influencing others is likability. In the group that got straight to business, 55 percent reached an agreement. In the group that took some time to connect on common ground or common goals, 90 percent closed a deal. This second group also managed to create outcomes that were typically worth more to both parties—further proof that taking the time to build a connection can go a long way. We tend to like people with whom we have something in common, people who pay genuine compliments before we get down to business, and people who are cooperative.

It isn't always about being the smartest in the room; maybe it is as much about emotional intelligence. Being likable, before you even start the actual negotiation, is worth the time and effort.

Practical Tips for Being Likable

Successful negotiations require keeping the conversation focused and moving forward. Here are some tips to make sure everyone stays fully engaged during your discussion.

- Make eye contact. Eye contact builds trust, as it demonstrates you are fully present. As a dear friend once told me, "When you look away, you give your power away."

- Smiling often signals openness. This small action can create a stronger sense of connection and put your partner more at ease.

- Consider your posture, your reactions, and your eye movement. One client of mine was told she would never get a promotion if she didn't stop rolling her eyes. Her reaction was, "What? I didn't say anything." Sometimes our nonverbals say more than we realize.

- Notice their emotional state. Pay attention to any emotions you might be picking up. If your partner seems frustrated or appears to be disengaging, it might be time for a break. Think about how your tone and words might be impacting your partner and adjust if necessary.

- Know your tone. Keep it strong yet pleasant, friendly yet firm, assertive and warm. In his book *Never Split the Difference*, Chris Voss suggests you can create a more soothing voice by dropping your chin.

- Slow the pace. A more deliberate pace can signal patience. Who doesn't want to negotiate with a patient partner?

- Pause. Make space for yourself to collect your thoughts and to allow the other person to jump in and share. Pauses are powerful! They give both parties a moment to think more deeply.

Trust Takes Time

Trust happens one conversation at a time and is the foundation of a strong relationship. It means taking the time to get to know your negotiation partner. Building relationships doesn't mean you have to roll out the therapy couch to learn everything about them. It does mean that you take the time to keep asking questions to connect at a deeper level. This holds especially true with negotiations. As Marshall Rosenberg writes in *Nonviolent Communication*, "People often need empathy and understanding before they are able to hear what is being said." You want to build a connection before you dive into the nitty-gritty aspects of the negotiation.

This reminds me of a simple sales model I learned early in my career: Relationship, Task, Relationship. The goal was to start every interaction with a personal connection, shift to focus on the task at hand, and end by doing something to reinforce your relationship.

This connection isn't a superficial gesture where you pretend you are interested in the other party; you really have to care and signal that care in a way that is obvious to your partner. You need to make them feel seen, heard, and respected. Like your comments when you reach out to set up the negotiations, your connection at the start of the conversation sets the tone for the rest of the negotiation.

If you did your homework to get to know your negotiation partner or learn something about them, this will be much easier. Start with some small talk or some schmoozing for a softer start. You want to make your partner feel safe around you. What do you know about the person that you could build on? What do you have in common? You can ask about their weekend or what they are most looking forward to this week.

If you don't know your potential negotiation partner, pay attention to the surroundings and what you notice the person doing. In my Birkenstock story, I noticed the salesclerk's behaviors. Ask them how they are doing today. What other questions might you ask them?

Finding Your Common Goal

My older daughter came home one day and announced, "Mom, I want to be a vegetarian." My gut reaction was "Great, how is that going to work when you don't like vegetables?" While thinking it, I knew this wasn't going to move the conversation forward. As the parent, I could have played the power card by demanding she just eat what I made or go hungry. However, I saw this as an opportunity to negotiate. The next chapter describes how this conversation went, so read on.

This whole conversation started when I asked my daughter about her day at school, which opened the door to the vegetarian conversation and eventually our negotiation. This was our first relationship moment. While it wasn't tied directly to the task at hand, it did start with the relationship framework.

To turn this into a negotiation, we needed to agree on what exactly we were negotiating. We needed to spend some time making sure we both had the same larger goal or were trying to solve the same problem, which we agreed was a healthy diet. This gave us something to work toward together rather than something to fight about. This is clarifying the task. If it is a planned negotiation, go back to your opening script about your objectives in chapter 4. Remember to introduce your topic by framing your goal in a way that identifies common ground with the other party. Alignment is crucial, or you could be moving in opposite directions.

Even when focused on the task, you want to demonstrate empathy and assertiveness. You demonstrate assertiveness by using the story you scripted and practiced earlier. You clearly state what you want, why, and how you can help the other side meet their needs. You demonstrate empathy by asking questions to make sure your partner is on the same page. Here's an example: "As I mentioned when we set up this meeting, I am concerned about the time required to deliver the quality of product you and the customer are used to. Right now, my plate is full, and I am not sure I can give the project the attention it needs. What are your thoughts? What options might we explore?"

If you are caught off guard by the conversation, like I was with my daughter, you will need to ask some questions to understand what is driving the conversation from their perspective. With the example of my daughter, we ultimately agreed that what we were talking about was a healthy diet and we just had different perspectives on how to get there.

Listening: Your Negotiation Superpower

No one is really asking if no one is really listening. No one cares about your position until they know you have heard and care about theirs. This means more than pretending to hear the words—it's about understanding the emotions, values, and hidden needs behind what is said.

One of the best ways to build and maintain a connection is to be fully present. Ideally your meeting location will make it easier for you both to stay focused and minimize interruptions. Below are some tips to be more intentional and focused.

- **Be fully present**: Give your partner 100 percent of your attention, which means eliminating all other distractions—especially electronics. As Susan Scott writes in her book *Fierce Conversations*, "Be here, prepared to be nowhere else."

- **Listen with all your senses**: What are their tone of voice and facial expressions telling you? Pay attention to their nonverbals, which often signal their emotional state beyond the words they use.

- **Don't interrupt**: Only one person should be talking at a time, so let your partner finish their thoughts.

- **Stay curious, not judgmental**: Try to keep an open mind. If you notice yourself slipping into judgment, you might ask for a break or refocus by asking your partner to repeat what they said in order to clarify. Remember that your goal is to figure out their "why."

- **Reflect and confirm**: Summarize what you heard in your own words to check you have understood your partner correctly. You want to paraphrase both content and emotions.
    - "It seems/sounds/looks/feels like you are most excited about the second option, as I noticed you were nodding your head and leaned forward. Did I get that right?"
    - If they say no: "What did I miss?"
    - If they say yes: "Great, tell me more."
    - Confirmation doesn't mean that you agree. It only validates that you heard them. And they won't hear you until you hear them.

- **Use the pause**: While the silence might feel awkward at first, it shows you are considering what they have said. A pause creates space for you to manage your emotions and really think about how you want to respond. It might also lead them to reveal more if they are uncomfortable with silence. Try, "Give me a minute to think about this."

- **Repair the listening gap**. If you do lose focus, own it.
    - "I got distracted thinking about your last point. Could you take me through that again?"
    - "I realize I missed part of your last comment. Could you repeat your point, so I fully understand your position?"
    - "Here's what I caught . . . What, if anything, did I miss?"

- Practice, practice, practice: Listening is like a muscle—it only improves with time, intention, and repetition.

When we ask our questions, we are obligated to listen carefully. Remember, negotiation isn't about winning—it's about building trust and collaboration. Listening at a deeper level can shift the negotiation from a tug-of-war to problem-solving partnership. The more you learn about your partner, the easier it will be to get past their objections.

Making a personal connection and building common ground will build the trust needed to carry you through the hard conversations to come. The stronger the relationship, the safer it is to dig deeper with more direct questions. Effective information exchange later in the process depends on our ability to make connections from the start. Beginning the negotiations with the goal of making both parties feel understood will keep you both focused when you start to explore your differences.

APPLY THE PRACTICE

Building Rapport

Before you start the actual negotiation, build rapport and strengthen the relationship. Difficult conversations can often be easier if you have built some trust beforehand.

- Who might you want to negotiate with in the future?

- How can you build a connection or relationship with this person?

- What are questions you could ask to build connection? (*"How was your vacation?" "What are you most looking forward to today?"*)

- What is one skill you can bring to increase your likability during the negotiation? (*eye contact, a smile, paying a genuine compliment, building on my partner's ideas with "yes, and," asking about their personal goals*)

Exercise: Identifying Shared Interests and Values

Map out your goals and your partner's goals, finding areas of overlap.

- Your Goals: List your primary objectives.

- Their Goals: Consider what the other party values most. "What is one thing you want to see happen today?"

- Common Goals: Identify where your goals overlap. What does a happy ending look like for everyone involved?

- Framing: How will you frame the common goal in your opening?

Listening Self-Check

Every stage you want to check in with yourself to see if you are really listening or just waiting to talk.

- Did I paraphrase what they said?

- Did I notice and acknowledge their emotions?

- Did I pause before responding?

- Did I demonstrate curiosity by asking more questions instead of giving my opinion?

Chapter 6

EXPLORE OPTIONS:
ASK, LISTEN, AND UNDERSTAND

"One of the best things you can do is stop and listen; that's why it's good to not just immediately respond when someone talks to you. Just stop and make sure you internalized what they said."

—Lori Richardson

You may recall I started a story in the last chapter about my daughter wanting to be a vegetarian. This could have turned into a heated argument had I assumed that the position she put on the table was the real issue. The reality is that the presented issue isn't always the real issue, and we often have to dig deeper to fully understand what is being negotiated.

Conversational Turn-Taking

In hopes of getting to the real issue and to show I valued her perspective, I asked my daughter, "Why don't you make a list telling me what's good about being a vegetarian and what's wrong with the way we eat now?" While she was completing her list, I was doing the same from the opposite perspective.

She came back with the benefits of being a vegetarian: It's better for the environment, it's healthier, and she wouldn't have to eat meat, which she didn't always like. Her cons for our current situation: I made weird food ("When my friends come over, why can't you make Krusteaz pancakes instead of lemon ricotta pancakes?"), and pork made her gag.

Ladies, LET'S NEGOTIATE

Next, it was my turn to share. I explained the pros of sticking with our current menu: There were four people in the house, three who seemed fine with my menus, and she needed protein as a growing teenager busy with sports. My cons for her argument were that she didn't like most vegetables, and being a vegetarian doesn't mean you're being healthy, plus it would be a lot more work for me to plan and cook vegetarian meals.

Truthfully, I didn't really have a problem with her being vegetarian. What parent doesn't want their kids to eat more vegetables? The real issues were becoming clear. My daughter didn't want me to cook pork anymore, and she wanted me to make more "normal" food when friends came over. My main issue was meal prep. These smaller issues were the real issues and seemed easier to negotiate than her being a vegetarian. (See the visual representation of our conversation below. My daughter's comments are in the darker boxes, and mine are in the lighter boxes.)

Healthy Diet

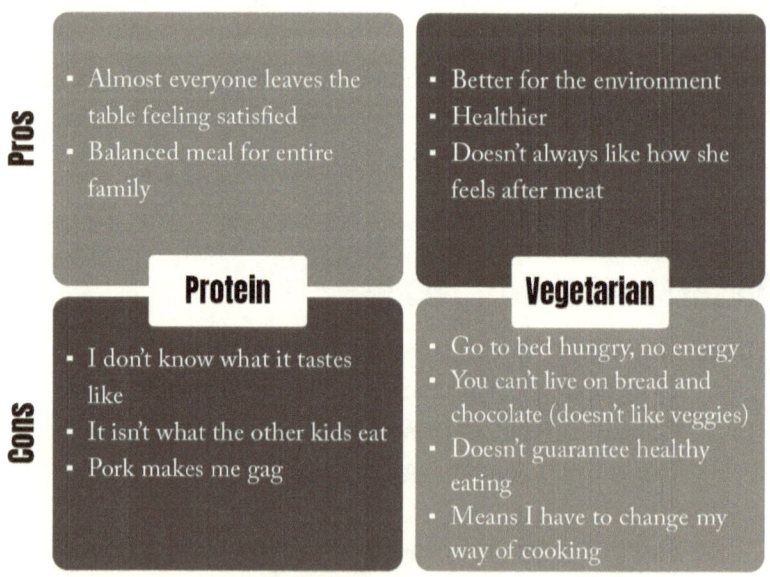

	Protein	**Vegetarian**
Pros	• Almost everyone leaves the table feeling satisfied • Balanced meal for entire family	• Better for the environment • Healthier • Doesn't always like how she feels after meat
Cons	• I don't know what it tastes like • It isn't what the other kids eat • Pork makes me gag	• Go to bed hungry, no energy • You can't live on bread and chocolate (doesn't like veggies) • Doesn't guarantee healthy eating • Means I have to change my way of cooking

I sent her to her room to brainstorm options that addressed both our issues. She came back and proposed spaghetti every day of the week, pizza once a week, and no pork ever. I countered with spaghetti once a week and pizza once every couple of weeks. My list included her going to the grocery store with me every week to pick out some protein substitutes and her picking out three vegetarian recipes every week. After watching me counter her offer, she agreed to go with me to the grocery store once a month and to pick out one recipe every week.

Our interaction is an example of conversational turn-taking. This is a simple technique that allows both sides to speak to their wants, needs, and issues. The process above really paints the picture of how people can present an issue that they want to negotiate but that's not really the true issue.

The Understanding Strategy—The Exploration Ask

Before we can claim value, we must create value. To do this, we have to know what the person across the table values and what they fear. We do that by practicing the 70/30 rule: spend 70 percent of your time asking questions and listening, and 30 percent talking.

The experience above highlights the importance of understanding the other person's position before you can focus on possible solutions.

Only when you understand the other person's position can you truly start negotiating. The *understanding strategy*, knowing what is important to the other person, has to happen before the *negotiation strategy*, the tactics you will use to advance the negotiations. The understanding strategy signals empathy and helps create value for both parties. We can't claim value for ourselves and move toward our goals before creating value for our partner by understanding their wants, needs, and interests/goals. To do this you need to clarify:

- **Needs**: the things they can't live without, their must-haves
- **Wants**: the things they want to have
- **Interests**: the why behind their wants and needs

- **Fears**: what they are protecting or the reason they are digging in

- **Decision-maker**: the person who has the power to decide, or access to that person

Use open-ended questions during these discussions. "What" and "how" questions tend to be more effective. "Who/when/where" are closed-ended questions and don't bring people into the conversation beyond basic facts or one-word answers. Questions that start with "why" can come across as defensive. "What" and "how" questions get the other person to share more deeply.

Try:

- "I want to be sure I have a clear picture of the pressures you face. What is behind your last point?"

- "Price is most important to me, as the project budget is tight. What issues are most important to you?"

- "I know you're balancing a lot of competing priorities here. How would you describe them?"

- "It seems/sounds/feels like something is bothering you. What feels at risk? What are you afraid of losing?"

Money Isn't the Only Thing That Matters

Even in sales, you have to determine what your partner values beyond the price. Keep asking questions and really listen to discover what else matters to your partner: expertise, convenience, reliability, simplification, flexibility, responsiveness, speed.

In my shoe shopping story from chapter 2, it was clear to me that the salesclerk *really* wanted to go home. He was sitting on the customer couch rubbing his forehead. Clearly quiet was more important than money, as he could have said "no" to my proposed deal. Pay attention to others' nonverbals and their mood.

Remember to consider the relationship. Does your negotiation partner feel valued, appreciated, respected, and important? Making connections contributes to likeability and flexibility, which also build trust. If trust is not there, do we really want to negotiate? Who are you more willing to negotiate with—someone you trust or someone you don't trust?

The Power of Persuasion

Persuasion is built on listening. Only when you truly listen can you validate someone else's perceptions. Their words and perceptions are more important than yours. What you say is less important than what they say. What you think you said is less important than what they think they've heard. It needs to be clear to them that you *heard* them.

When you ask questions, reflect on what you heard:

- "It seems/sounds/feels/looks like option B best meets your needs, as you lit up when we discussed it. Did I get that right?"
- If no: "What did I miss?"
- If yes: "Great—what would make it even better?"

Share Information

You may recall the concept of the meeting before the meeting, where you introduce the idea of the negotiation. Just as you started the conversation, you can be the one to set the tone for being transparent. Once you share, the rules of reciprocity kicks in. Talking about your interests shows that you trust them. If you share, others are also likely to share if you give them time and space without interrupting them or making it all about you.

The Power of Silence

Some people are uncomfortable with silence. Yet while negotiating, silence can be your friend. After you ask a question, give the other person time to consider their response without jumping in. If you have been given new information, take time to absorb the content. Take some deep breaths and manage your emotions. Think about how you want to respond in a productive manner.

Imagine trying to solve a puzzle without all the pieces—it's frustrating. Negotiation is the same thing; you never have a complete picture if you don't have all the pieces. Your pieces are gathered by asking questions that go deeper than the surface. It's not about prying; it's about understanding. The more you know about what drives the other side, the better your chances are of finding a solution that works for both of you. So next time you're in a negotiation, pretend you are looking for the missing piece of the puzzle. Ask, listen, pause, and piece together the clues. You'll be amazed at what you discover.

APPLY THE PRACTICE

Exploring with Curiosity—The Understanding Strategy

Your primary objective at this point is information exchange to make sure you fully understand the other person's perspective. It is unlikely your partner will listen to you until they feel fully heard by you.

Exploratory, Open-Ended Questions

Pinpoint common goals or interests to keep the negotiation collaborative.

- What's most important to you in this negotiation?
- What concerns do you have, and how can we address them?
- What shared goals do we have? (*project success, team stability, mutual respect*)
- How can we both benefit from finding an agreement? (*"We both want what's best for the company; let's find a way to make this work." My kids helping with the chores allowed us to share more fun time together.*)
- What are potential areas of compromise that benefit both sides?
- What would your ideal outcome look like?

Use the conversational turn-taking worksheet below to help you identify real issues. Once you have the issues on the table, the goal is to determine the importance of each want, need, and issue.

APPLY THE PRACTICE

COMMON GOAL	
What is working with your idea or approach? (You complete.)	What is working with their idea or approach? (Partner completes.)
What isn't working with your idea or approach? (Partner completes.)	What isn't working with their idea or approach? (You complete.)

Listening Prompts

- Summarize. (*"It seems/sounds/feels like _____ is your most important need."*)

- Ask open-ended questions to further clarify. (*"What's driving that need?"*)

- Pause before responding. (*Count to three silently after they speak.*)

Chapter 7
ADVANCE YOUR ASK:
MOVE FORWARD WITH CONFIDENCE

> "Everything is negotiable. Whether or not the negotiation is easy is another thing."
> —CARRIE FISHER

Remember when you learned to drive? Most of us didn't learn to drive on a freeway with seven lanes going each direction. Typically, we started on a country road or parking lot just to figure out the mechanics of driving. Along the way, we also learned the basics of driving, such as how to read traffic signs, how to choose the right lane, how to change lanes, how to match your speed to traffic flow, drivers' etiquette such as looking left-right-left, and so on. This is the prep work you did, along with hours of practice, before jumping on the seven-lane freeway.

Navigating the Unpredictability of Negotiations

Negotiations are like driving. You prepare yourself, set the stage, open the conversation, and start asking questions, hoping to move fully into the actual negotiations. But like with driving, you have no idea what the other person is going to do. Slowdowns happen due to construction zones, weather condition shifts, accidents, or animals crossing the road. Yet you still have to get to your destination, constantly making adjustments along the way.

You have to realize that you don't have full control over the situation. You have to rely on your upfront work and stay flexible. Progress doesn't mean controlling the conversation and outcome; it means making adjustments along the way to get to your shared goal. There will no doubt be twists and turns, but if you set the stage, open the conversation, identify the real issues, and stay focused on common ground, you will continue to move the negotiation forward.

Emotions Matter: Staying Centered When the Conversation Gets Messy

Negotiation isn't just about logic; it's about people. People don't check their emotions at the door when they negotiate; emotions are always in the room, both yours and theirs. Women typically are better at recognizing the emotions of those around them, which is good and bad.

Emotions are often seen as a weakness in negotiation. Yet those who can read the room by picking up on shifts in energy, body language, and tone will connect more deeply. We might be able to pick up the emotions that allow us to see aspects of the negotiation that others might miss.

While we have been taught to handle difficult reactions to keep the conversation going, we sometimes worry too much about how others might feel or how negotiations might impact the relationship. The goal is to recognize that as humans, we will always have emotions—but that doesn't mean our emotions should have us (the prep work in chapter 2). The goal isn't to erase emotions; it's to use emotional information to your advantage. That's where the following framework comes in.

Space, Pace, and Grace

One of my favorite frameworks for dealing with difficult conversations, which often arise during negotiations, is Space, Pace, and Grace. This simple approach can help you stay grounded and productive during tough moments.

Space: Every action creates a reaction, which impacts your interaction. Give yourself room to breathe. Recognize your hot buttons, or triggers that set you off, and do what it takes to calm yourself. Pause before you react by taking a breath, practicing your mantra, getting a drink of water, and letting the emotion wash over you. Remind yourself that emotions are signals, not facts. You don't have to act on every feeling.

Pace: Slow down the pace of the conversation by asking thoughtful questions to make sure you understand the real issues. Adding even a few seconds to the conversation can reduce reactivity, allow you to collect your thoughts so you respond respectfully, and give the other person a chance to share more of what's really going on for them. Pace communicates patience, which can calm a frustrated partner.

Grace: Extend understanding—even when the other person isn't. Maintain a respectful tone to make the other person feel heard. Repeat back what you've heard, find areas of agreement, and build on the positives. Instead of criticizing, practice building your collaboration skills. Reframe judgment as curiosity. Use statements like the following:

- "Here's what I'm hearing."
- "It sounds like this is important to you."
- "Let's figure this out together."
- "It seems like this deal makes you uneasy."

Show respect without shrinking. Hold your ground without hostility. It's not about giving in; it's about staying in the conversation with integrity.

Compassion, Respect, and Humor

It is easy to slip into bad behavior when your partner does, yet there are better options. Don't assume it is your fault that they are in a bad mood. If they're short or reactive, it doesn't mean you did something wrong.

If the other person doesn't demonstrate any flexibility or appears angry, consider what might be driving their behavior. We are all messy humans with messy lives. Maybe your partner is gripped by fear of not getting what they want or think they need. Instead of escalating, de-escalate. Keep your tone calm. Make eye contact.

Showing a bit of empathy and humor might reduce their resistance and make it easier to move forward together. Appropriate humor can be a release valve—*a reminder that you're both human, not adversaries.*

When the other person feels seen and respected, they're more likely to relax, listen, and collaborate. That's the win.

Mastering Yourself First

When the conversation gets tough, remember that the only person you can change is yourself. You can't control how the other person reacts—but you *can* control how you respond.

Stay composed. Even if you are nervous, try to keep your voice even, watch your word choices, and avoid filler words. Circle back to shared values and stay focused on the bigger picture. Be approachable but firm. Be kind and have a spine.

Remember, nothing derails a negotiation faster than someone losing control of their emotions. The more you manage your reactions, the more likely it is you will keep the conversation going. Managing your inner world so you can navigate the outer one with clarity and confidence is a fundamental key in negotiations.

Tactics When Things Get Tough

Things might hit a standstill, or you might notice your partner losing interest. Should that happen, you might consider the following tactics.

Bundling

One way to move negotiations forward is by bundling—combining multiple items into a single offer. That is why you need to understand your options and what leverage you might have in a situation. This can make an offer more appealing, especially if you have something of interest to them that isn't that important to you.

For example, if you can't get a higher salary, you might negotiate for flexible work hours, additional development opportunities, or a different bonus structure. If you are buying a car, you might be willing to pay more in exchange for free oil changes or an extended warranty. Bundling gives you some flexibility to hopefully move you closer to a win-win outcome.

Standards

Are there standards that apply to this situation, such as industry norms or quality guarantees? When standards exist, they give you some credibility and leverage.

For example, Costco offers a 100 percent satisfaction guarantee, allowing members to return almost any product at any time for a full refund. Think about it: Is there a warranty, a commitment, or an expectation that you can hold the other person to in your negotiation? It is also about making sure you get what you deserve, because that is what was promised. Standards can shift the conversation from a personal desire to an objective fact. For instance, "According to a recent market study, roles like mine typically pay X. I would love to be in alignment with fair market value."

Ask yourself these questions:

- What standards, norms, and benchmarks do you have in hand to support your ask?

- How can you present that information in a way that seems fair to both parties?

- How can you share this information, linking it to the norm, to make your point more compelling?

Reframing

If negotiations stall, try to reframe the issue. The goal is to turn a negative into a positive. This often requires going back to the things that you openly agree on. For example, if your boss said, "We can't afford raises for anyone right now," instead of objecting, you might reframe with "I understand the budget is tight. What could I do to better position myself for a raise when the budget improves? Could we consider a promotion or a development opportunity?" Reframing keeps the conversation going by exploring other options.

Incremental Change

When you know it might not be possible to get what you really want, look for a small win to build some momentum.

For example, if your laptop breaks just after the warranty expires, demanding a free replacement might not work. Instead, you could ask for a discount on a new laptop, free or discounted repairs, or an extended service plan. You can keep the negotiations going if you ask for something more realistic.

- How can you break down your wishes or proposal into smaller, bite-sized options?

- How might you shift your timeline incrementally if nothing else can change?

- Ask, "What small change could we agree to right now?"

Make Them the Expert

One way to shift the energy in a negotiation is to ask your partner for advice. It flatters the other person, signals you're open to their ideas, and strengthens the relationship. It can also give you more options you hadn't considered.

Approaching the situation as a problem to be solved can change the dynamic from defensive to productive. Instead of pushing, pull them into exploring additional options. Use three-word sentences to make them feel safe to lean into the negotiation.

- "I'm not sure."

- "I was wrong."

- "I don't know."

- "Tell me more."

Make Small Concessions

Negotiation works only when both parties see a willingness to give rather than just take. To move forward, both you and your partner need to feel you are gaining something of value. The challenge is balancing what you are willing to give with what you expect in return. Give-and-take isn't about giving in; it's about making thoughtful trade-offs that align with your shared goals and move you closer to your Zone of Possible Agreement (ZOPA).

This is where preparation matters. Go back to your list:

- What are your must-haves versus nice-to-haves?

- Where can you be flexible?

- What are potential areas where they might be willing to give?

Knowing this ahead of time helps you stay focused and can give you ideas for your next move. For example, when buying a mattress, you may agree to a slightly higher price if it includes a mattress pad, a free pillow, or a discount on some other item in the store. You give a little, but you also gain something in exchange.

That's the key: If you start giving without getting something in return, you're heading down a slippery slope. If you concede too quickly or too often, your partner might question whether you really know what you want or if you are firm on anything. Every concession should be intentional and met with something of value in return. If not, you could end up hurting both your results and relationship, as you may resent the final deal.

If you find your partner unwilling to concede, shift back to asking questions. You may not have truly identified, much less addressed, their core needs, wants, or interests. Also consider going back to your shared goals. The best negotiations aren't about winning or losing—they're about finding solutions where both parties leave the table with something they value.

Because requests or options might come up that you hadn't considered, you might need to take a break to rethink your options. Rarely can we make a deal in our first meeting, as so much of that meeting is about collecting information and building trust. So don't be afraid to ask for another meeting or a break. That is far better than giving in just for the sake of getting the deal done. Short-term relief from being done with negotiating can cost you long-term success in strong results and relationships. Know that if your partner refuses to give on any aspect of the deal, it may be time to walk away.

Growth Mindset

A great negotiator doesn't get stuck in either-or thinking. Rather, they look for possibilities.

Once when I was cooking with my daughter, we both needed a lemon. Unfortunately, there was only one in the house. If I had decided either she got it or I got it, one of us might not have been able to finish our part of the meal. Instead, we discussed what the other person needed the lemon for. She needed the lemon juice for a sauce, and I wanted the zest for baking. Because we took the time to understand each other's needs, we both got what we needed.

We all have different needs and emotions. Better negotiators do better for themselves *and* their counterparts so both can win! When you understand the other person's true need, you can be creative in finding a solution.

Remember, negotiation is about balancing relationships, results, and respect for all parties involved. If you focus too much on relationships, you may end up pleasing others at your own expense. Know your worth, hold your boundaries, and remember that without give-and-take on both sides, you run the risk of resentment and little follow-through.

When You Get Stuck

There are going to be times things stall. When you see this happening, recognize there needs to be some type of shift, in meeting time, meeting place, focus, or something else. If you are still feeling stuck after a break, you might try working backward from your common goals.

- Share your observation about their behavior. (*"When I said X, your body language changed."*)

- Identify their perceived need or want. (*"This suggests that this point is really important to you."*)

- Propose an action that addresses their concern. (*"Would you prefer/like . . . ?"*)

- Ask clarifying questions. (*"What's non-negotiable for you?"*, *"Which part of this matters most to you?"*, or *"What would make you feel comfortable moving forward?"*)

- Use conditional statements. (*"If you ____, then I ____."* Example: *"If you handle X, I can take care of Y."*)

- Encourage mutual brainstorming. (*"I have a few ideas on how we can move forward. I'd love to hear yours before I share mine. Hopefully, among all the options, we can find one that works for both of us."*)

- Continue to foster safety. (*"Let's go back to your last offer. Which item do you still want to see progress?"*)

If you are still feeling stuck after trying the items above, you might need another break or change of scenery. Before throwing in the towel, always go back over your areas of agreement to show you are making progress, which might provide you with some energy to tackle the next point.

Concessions You Should Avoid

While concessions are normal in negotiations, some concessions should never be made:

- Don't start with the minimum you'll accept. That leaves you no room to negotiate.

- Avoid concessions that leave you feeling resentful. If you start to feel that resentment creep in, you may not have explored enough options.

- Don't split the difference too quickly, especially if you've already conceded more than your partner.

- Never concede out of fear or exhaustion. If you feel pressured, take a break to regroup and recharge.

Avoiding Language That Undermines Your Credibility

Women in particular tend to use language that marginalizes their contributions. Try to avoid the following to better maintain your credibility:

- "I **just** did it to help." → Take credit where credit is due: "I noticed this was a problem and took action to correct it."

- "I **supported** the project." → Be clear about your role: "I played a key role in organizing the team and ensuring we met deadlines."

- "It was **luck**." → Acknowledge your effort: "My hard work positioned me for this opportunity."

Think about it: How have you felt when you made everyone else happy at your own expense? Did this help you get the best results for everyone? Did it really strengthen your relationships, or did it leave you feeling resentful? You have to respect yourself as much you respect your partner.

APPLY THE PRACTICE

Tools for Advancing the Discussion

Remember, your primary goal is to advocate for yourself. Before you start advancing, remind yourself of your priorities.

Reflection

- What are your nonnegotiables (needs) versus those points you can be more flexible around (wants)?

- When are you most likely to concede or give in without getting something in return?

- How do you manage your short-term desires (just getting the deal done) with your long-term goals?

- What is your typical reaction when the other party won't budge? What tactics might you try to shift the conversation?

- What's one way you can stand your ground around your needs in your next negotiation without giving too much away?

Try these techniques to keep the conversation going and advance your negotiation strategy.

Bundling

- **Exercise:** Create a bundled offer using the information you developed in chapter 3, adding the information gathered during your discussion to create a more attractive proposal.

Standards

- What industry or organizational standards might apply in this situation?

- What standards, norms, and benchmarks do you have in hand to support your ask?

- How can you present that information in a way that seems fair to both parties?

- How can you share this information, linking it to the norm, to make your point more compelling?

Reframe Objections

- Example: "It's too expensive." Try instead: "I understand the concern about cost—let's look at the long-term savings."

- "Why won't you give a little?" Try, "It sounds like you've been burned before. What are you most concerned about losing?"

Incremental Changes

- How can you break down your wishes or proposal into smaller, bite-sized options?

- "What elements, such as timing, scope, or outcomes, could be incrementally adjusted?"

- Ask, "What small change could we agree to right now?"

Make Them the Expert

- Ask, "How might I do that?" or "If you were in my shoes, what would you do?"

- "What would the perfect deal look like for both parties from your perspective?"

Making Concessions

- Review your list of must-haves versus nice-to-haves.

- Consider where you could be more flexible given what you have learned.

- Always remember to ask, "Where are you willing to give?"

Chapter 8

REJECTION:
NAVIGATE THE "NO"

"Personally, I've learned about perseverance: When you hear the word "no," and when you hear rejection, that it's not always final."

—Angela Robinson

Last year I was working with an organization doing a Teamwork Bootcamp series. Originally the sessions were all set up to be virtual due to budget constraints. Given the learning outcomes desired by the client, I pitched an additional workshop to be done in person. They loved the idea yet knew it had to be approved at a higher level. Unfortunately, the answer was still no.

I could have left that meeting thinking that the bonus session was a pipe dream. But instead, I took a breath and asked, "What would need to change for this to become a reality for you?"

Given that the organization was being acquired, everything was under the microscope when it came to budgets. Thus, I understood the response that all travel was on hold for another year. I thanked her for her honesty and said, "I completely understand. If things change, I'd love to revisit this conversation."

About five months later, another client asked me to do some work not more than an hour away from the organization for which I was doing the webinars. I reached out to see if we might be able to do the additional session live if there were no travel expenses beyond one night's hotel. This changed everything, and we found our way to a "yes."

Had I walked away from the deal without thinking about other options, we might never have added that last session. If you keep your eyes and ears open, you might find a way to get the "yes" you are looking for down the road.

"No" Doesn't Mean "Never"

Let's get one thing straight: "no" doesn't always mean the conversation is over. "No" often just means "not yet." Somewhere along the way, I was taught that "no" was a request for more information. Maybe it is just a "not right now" or "not in this way" type of response.

When learning to negotiate, expect rejection—often. But what is the worst thing that can happen if you ask or start negotiations? As I told my kids, the worst thing that can happen is your partner will say "no," which is the same thing that is happening if you don't ask. Yet the best thing that could happen is they might actually give you what you want or some concession, which is better than nothing. Even if the answer is "no" in the moment, the conversation might plant a seed for a future conversation or a "yes."

A great TED Talk that makes this point is "What I Learned in 100 Days of Rejection." The speaker, Jia Jiang, put himself in situations where rejection was likely. He did this to get more comfortable with rejection and to see if he could reframe the rejection into an opportunity. His key takeaways were that every rejection is a chance to shift your ask, better understand the other person's needs, and try again—often with different outcomes.

Rejection is rarely personal, just a response to a specific request at this specific time. Your response to rejection determines whether it's a dead end or a detour to reaching your goals.

Ask: What Would It Take to Get a "Yes"?

Instead of shutting down after a "no," move into the conversation with curiosity.

- "What made that offer difficult for you to accept?"
- "What needs of yours aren't being met?"
- "What might you be willing to accept?"

Often a rejection is just a request for more information, so questions show you're serious! They shift the conversation from ending back into exploring. For example, if your request for coaching is rejected due to budget issues, consider asking what it would take to include it in next year's budget. Then remember to follow up to make sure it gets on the budget and that you are first in line for the development dollars.

If your salary negotiations stall, look beyond pay. Could you negotiate additional leave time, tuition reimbursement, or a flexible work arrangement? Having more options makes it easier to come up with creative solutions that meet everyone's needs.

Don't Take "No" as the Final Answer

A "no" doesn't have to be the end; in fact, it can be the real start to the actual negotiation. Stay engaged and confident in your request. If the answer is "no" today, what would need to change for it to be "yes" next time? Go back to asking "what" and "how" questions to find why you were turned down. Ask your negotiation partner what it would take next time.

Consider asking these questions:

- "You said you couldn't do this. What is preventing you?"
- "If I came back in six months, what would you want to see changed?"
- "You mentioned your budget limits. What might we be able to barter to help each other move this forward?"
- "What moves would you suggest to help me gain new skills for future opportunities?"

- "Could I get additional training to address those needs?"

Shifting gears gives you more leverage for future negotiations.

If you get stuck in traffic, you don't stop driving—you find a new route. The same applies to negotiation. If you're stuck, back up or take an exit ramp, adjust your approach, and ask your partner their thoughts on what it would take to move forward.

- "What would need to happen to create movement?"

- "How could we approach this differently to see if you can make some progress?"

Drawing your partner into problem-solving validates their role and keeps them engaged in finding a solution.

When "No" Is the Final Answer

At some point, "no" means "no." When you reach that point, it is time to respectfully step back.

- Acknowledge their position: "I understand your perspective."

- End on a positive note: "Thank you for the conversation. I appreciate you considering my ask."

Manage Your Emotions When Rejected

Have your emotions, or they will have you. We all know rejections can sting. How do you prepare yourself when things aren't going your way or you feel you have just lost your way in the conversation? Here are some strategies to stay grounded:

- Go back to the work you did in the planning process. Remind yourself why you're negotiating in the first place.

- Take a break. It is okay to ask for a break, or set up another meeting, if you need some space.

- Don't forget to breathe. Think about your mantra. Remember that rejection is a fleeting moment. Stay focused so you respond rather than react.

Reject an Offer Yourself

Don't forget there are two people at the table, and it might be you rejecting the offers from your partner. If an offer doesn't meet your needs, be thoughtful in your response.

The Kenyan Kamba proverb "Kumawa nikusyokawa" translates to "A point of departure is also returned to." You have to be thoughtful in how you state your rejections because you want to leave a good name in case you return.

Space, Pace, and Grace When You Have to Say "No"

- Space: Give your partner some time to process your decision. Allow enough time for them to ponder options and deal with the rejection.

- Pace: Ask another question.
    - "To make that work, would you consider . . . ?"
    - "How might you feel if this was the offer you got?"
    - "How close can you get to this option?"

- Grace: State your position in a positive way. "That is a stretch for me. [pause] Here is what I can do . . ." instead of "I can't do that."

Your reputation will precede you. How you reject an offer affects that reputation. If you want to keep the door open for future conversations, remember to practice Space, Pace, and Grace while maintaining your boundaries.

Rejection is part of the process that no one escapes. Yet every "no" gets you closer to a "yes." The more comfortable you get with rejection, the more likely you will be to lean into future opportunities.

Your ability to stay strong and demonstrate respectful behavior will help create a reputation that will serve you well in future negotiations. Instead of fearing rejection, remember to give yourself a huge pat on the back for staying in there and maintaining your composure. This time it might be "no," but maybe this "no" is the one that gets you one step closer to your "yes." Remember, the goal is to move from fear to fair.

If you really think you deserve more and are continuously turned down, it might be time to start looking for other options.

APPLY THE PRACTICE

Handling Rejection—Navigating the "No"

Rejection Resilience Plan

- How do you typically respond to rejection?
- How can you reframe a "no" into a future opportunity?
- What's one way you can stay focused on your goal after an initial rejection?

Don't Take "No" as the Final Answer

A "no" doesn't have to be the end; it can actually be the start of the real negotiating. Consider asking questions like the following:

- "If I wanted to come back in six months to try again, what would you need to see changed to reopen the conversation?"
- "You mentioned budget limits. What might we be able to barter to move this conversation forward?"
- "If I can't get a raise, would you be willing to give me a promotion? What additional skills might I need to make this a reality? What options do I have to acquire those skills?"

Closing the Conversation

- "I appreciate your feedback. When might be a good time to revisit this?"
- "Thank you for the opportunity to discuss—I appreciate your willingness to consider my perspective."

PART 3

Close

The deal isn't really done until you follow through and take the time to reflect on the lessons you learned along the way.

Chapter 9

SEALING THE DEAL:
FINALIZE AGREEMENTS

"You don't close a sale; you open a relationship if you want to build a long-term, successful enterprise."

—Patricia Fripp

On a holiday flight to Phoenix to visit family, I got the middle seat between a couple. When I boarded the plane, they were actually sitting together, so I asked if they wanted to switch seats. The response was "No, we have been married for forty years, so we have had plenty of time to talk to each other." They moved to their seats, and I took the middle seat.

As soon as the doors on the plane closed and they couldn't text each other, they started talking over me. I offered to change seats, and again they said, "No thanks." I told them I had some work to do, so I took out my laptop and put on my headphones.

Then they started passing their phones with messages on them, behind my laptop. Again, I offered to give them the middle seat, and they finally agreed that might be best, as something had come up they needed to discuss. I said, "Great, how about I take the window seat?" They hesitated and stated they would prefer to have the window and middle seat and tried to convince me I would have more leg room in the aisle seat.

I reminded myself that in closing a deal, you need to ask for what you really want. The first time I asked, I might have agreed to take the aisle. Now I knew I had more leverage to ask for what I wanted. I was polite and clear about my preferences. Eventually they gave me the window seat, they got to have their conversation, and I was finally able to get some work done.

Closing the Deal with Confidence

You have done the hard work—preparing, problem-solving, and making trade-offs—and you can almost see the finish line. To wrap this deal up, you still need to nail down the final details to ensure things go as planned. Closing isn't just getting to "yes"; it is making sure you have built in accountability and follow-through.

Finalizing Details

Now is the time to check to see if you have missed anything.

- **Clarify commitments**: Make sure everyone understands what they have agreed to—who is doing what, by when, and how success will be measured.

- **Identify potential barriers**: What could get in the way of implementation? Organizational change? Shifts in the economy? Your partner taking a new job?

- **Confirm your next steps**: Outline your timelines, owners, next steps, accountabilities, and check-ins.

- **Get it in writing**: Getting it in writing is more than a formality—it's the moment where clarity becomes commitment. It signals that both parties are ready to move from talk to action.

- **Express gratitude**: Always thank your partner for their effort, even if you didn't get exactly what you wanted.

If you build trust and understanding and maintain a good relationship, you have made progress. Thank them for their time, effort, and commitment. For example: "Thanks for taking the time to work through this with me. I am looking forward to seeing how this all works out and to working with you on this as it progresses." Even if the other individual could have been more supportive, set the tone for how you want to be remembered.

There Is More at Stake Than the Deal

Closing might feel like the end, but it's really the beginning of putting the agreement into action. By taking the time to review the key points, ensure understanding, and plan next steps, you improve the odds of seeing the plan put into action. You have to make sure the deal sticks and relationships stay intact.

Think of this as framing the puzzle. You've worked through the challenging parts and put the major pieces into place, and now it's time to step back and see the big picture. Remind yourself, "We did it!" and look forward to seeing the final fruits of your labor.

APPLY THE PRACTICE

Closing and Follow-Up

The deal isn't done until it is implemented. Ensure all points are clear and commitments are solid.

Summarize Key Points

- Make a final pass on agreed terms and confirm understanding.

- Confirm who has agreed to what, and by when.

- Clarify terms of the deal such as price, scope, quantity, and quality.

- Nail down deadlines and milestones.

- Discuss possible problems, such as market or organizational changes or job loss. Ask, "Is there something else I need to know, or that we might have missed? What could change that would snag this deal?"

- Gauge motivation: Even if someone has the ability to do something, will they be motivated to do it? Ability doesn't always ensure follow-through. "What has you most excited about this? What might reduce that excitement?"

- Put the agreement into writing and have both parties sign it.

Create a Follow-Up Plan

- Outline your follow-up schedule with action items, check-ins, and deadlines.

- Consider action plans and contacts if things aren't going as expected.

Chapter 10
FOLLOW-THROUGH AND REFLECTION:
BUILD SKILLS FOR NEXT TIME

> "It's through reflection and learning from each negotiation that we refine our strategies and strengthen our resolve."
> —WENDY SHERMAN

When I accepted a new job at a bank, part of my agreement included a part-time summer schedule so I could spend more time with my kids when they were out of school. Everyone agreed we could figure out a way to make this work, and I assumed it would just happen. Well, we all know what happens when we assume.

About a month before summer break, I walked into my boss's office to discuss how we would work out the summer plan. He blankly looked at me and said, "We can't do that in the middle of a system conversion." I had assumed the deal was set in stone—that there weren't going to be exceptions.

Lessons I learned:

- Check in early and often. Don't assume the details will take care of themselves.

- Trust and verify. If you didn't get everything in writing, you might be renegotiating.

Had I started the conversation sooner, I might have had more leverage. At least the lesson wasn't wasted, and by sharing this, I hope you won't make the same mistake. Closing the deal means capturing the agreement. Following through means honoring it. Always honor your end and do what you can to make your negotiation partner honor theirs.

Keep the Momentum Going!

Even after an agreement is reached, watch for any wavering by your partner. Some of this is natural—don't we all have doubts before committing to something? Second-guessing happens, so do what you can to keep things on track.

- Ease those doubts by reviewing your purpose: Remind your partner why this agreement benefits both sides. "Let's just take one last look at what we accomplished and why it worked for us."

- Continue to watch for barriers: "Let's brainstorm possible obstacles."

- Do a motivational check-in: It never hurts to follow up to make sure nothing significant has changed. You don't want to wait until it is too late to do anything.

Follow-Through, the Key to Credibility

Why negotiate if you aren't going to hold people accountable? Your credibility depends on follow-through on your end of the agreement as well as your partner's.

Deals fall apart when follow-up is neglected. If you've agreed to do anything, you must follow through on your end. If other people have agreed to do something, you need to hold them accountable. Once people know you don't necessarily follow through with yourself or with others, they aren't likely to hold up their end of the bargain.

Reflect

Reflection isn't just for meditation—it is a critical part of becoming a stronger negotiator. Pro athletes watch game videos to reflect and learn from every game. Negotiators should review their conversations too.

After every negotiation, take time to reflect and ask yourself these questions:

- What worked well?

- What didn't work well or go as planned?

- What surprised you in the process?

- What might you do differently next time? What else might you try?

- What goals might you set for the next negotiation?

- How can you find meaning in failure? Don't get stuck in the "why me" destructive loop.

Keep going back to "What did I learn from this experience?" Go back to curiosity and grace for yourself. This is the key to building your skills and your resilience. You don't need a perfect outcome; you need the willingness to step back and learn.

Track Your Progress

If you want to grow as a negotiator, document your growth. A few notes after each negotiation can reveal powerful patterns over time.

- **Record what happened.** Who did you negotiate with? What did you negotiate? What was the result?

- **Note your emotional state.** How did you feel going in, and how did you feel coming out?

- **Capture one key insight.** What lesson did you take away? How will you apply it going forward?

Negotiation isn't a one-and-done skill—it's a lifelong practice. Every conversation is a chance to get better, braver, and more intentional.

Find Opportunities for Feedback

If you want to keep improving, set up some time with your negotiating partner or others involved to get their feedback and suggestions.

- Who might have some insights?

- How did you feel about the experience, and which area of feedback most interests you: your negotiation style; the questions you used; your composure; word choices; tone; body language.

Develop a Plan

Like any skill, negotiation isn't about perfection; it's about progress. Use what you've learned to tweak your approach going forward.

Keep Going

Congratulations on making it to the end of the book! Really, this is just the start. Remember that negotiation is a lifelong skill, and the more you practice, the more comfortable you become and the better you get. The goal isn't to be perfect—it's to learn to negotiate to get more of what you want out of life. You don't become a confident negotiator all at once; it happens with one risk, one conversation, and one reflection at a time.

Prepare, practice, progress, and prosper!

APPLY THE PRACTICE

Reflection and Goal Setting

Accountability

- How do you hold others accountable for agreements?
- If you don't, why don't you? (See chapter 2.)
- If you typically hold people accountable, where have you let follow-through slip?

Post-Negotiation Reflection

- What went well?
- What surprised you?
- What did you learn from this experience?
- What will you do differently next time?
- How will you use this experience to keep growing?

Ask Others for Input

- Who else might you ask for insights on how the negotiation went?
- What suggestions might they have for you to move forward?

Final Thought

Remember, every negotiation is a chance to learn and build the life you deserve. Keep practicing, keep reflecting, and keep growing. You've got this—now go make it happen!

WORKS CITED

Cialdini, Robert B. *Influence: The Psychology of Persuasion.* Harper Business, 2021.

Davidds, Yasmin. *Your Own Terms: A Woman's Guide to Taking Charge of Any Negotiation.* AMACOM, 2015.

Jiang, Jia. "What I Learned from 100 Days of Rejection." *TEDx Talks*, January 6, 2017. YouTube, 15:31. https://www.youtube.com/watch?v=-vZXgApsPCQ.

Melbourne Institute and Roy Morgan. "Women Continue to Do More Unpaid Domestic Work than Men, Better Provision of External Support Services and Greater Flexibility to Work from Home Needed to Reduce Burden" May 1, 2023. https://www.roymorgan.com/findings/women-continue-to-do-more-unpaid-domestic-work-than-men-better-provision-of-external-support-services-and-greater-flexibility-to-work-from-home-needed-to-reduce-burden.

National Partnership for Women & Families. "America's Women and the Wage Gap." October 2025. https://nationalpartnership.org/wp-content/uploads/2023/02/americas-women-and-the-wage-gap.pdf.

Rosenberg, Marshall B. *Nonviolent Communication: A Language of Life.* PuddleDancer Press, 2015.

Scott, Susan. *Fierce Conversations: Achieving Success at Work and in Life One Conversation at a Time.* Berkley, 2004.

US Bureau of Labor Statistics. "Women's Earnings Were 83.6 Percent of Men's in 2023." *TED: The Economics Daily.* March 12, 2024. https://www.bls.gov/opub/ted/2024/womens-earnings-were-83-6-percent-of-mens-in-2023.htm.

Voss, Chris, and Tahl Raz. *Never Split the Difference: Negotiating as If Your Life Depended on It.* Harper Business, 2016.

ABOUT THE AUTHOR

Nan Gesche, MA, is a communication expert with over twenty years of experience helping clients collaborate better so they can achieve more. Nan has an MA in Organizational Communications, a professional certificate in Training & Development, and is a trusted partner to Fortune 500 companies and national organizations. She also teaches leadership and communication at the University of Minnesota (including the Carlson School of Management) and the Graduate School of Banking in Madison.

As a speaker, educator, and consultant, Nan challenges clients to rethink how they communicate and lead. Her goal is to build collaboration skills to work through challenging conversations and problem-solving so people can get back to the business of reaching their goals while strengthening relationships.

Nan is qualified to administer and train in the Myers-Briggs Type Indicator, ExperienceChange™, the Conflict Dynamics Profile, and the Life Styles Inventory. Nan is also a member of the Minnesota and National Speakers Association.

To book a workshop, training session, or keynote experience, visit nangesche.com.

www.ingramcontent.com/pod-product-compliance
Lightning Source LLC
Chambersburg PA
CBHW030838180526
45163CB00004B/1374